The Spirit-Filled Life

The
Spirit-Filled
Life

by

John MacNeil

MOODY PRESS

CHICAGO

MOODY PRESS EDITION
1984
1 2 3 4 5 6 7 Printing DB Year 88 87 86 85 84

ISBN:0-8024-0493-6

Printed in the United States of America

The following prefaced the 1895 edition.—Ed.

How to Use This Book

A FEW SUGGESTIONS

Peruse it for personal pleasure and profit.

Read it aloud to the young folks.

Use it for reading lessons with the children, or foreigners seeking a better knowledge of English.

Present it to the grocer's boy, milkman or someone calling at your door.

Keep it and others circulating as a library.

Offer it and others as rewards to Sunday school scholars for punctuality, regularity or for the memorizing of Scripture, etc.

Forward it to a lumber camp or prison, the sailors, soldiers, firemen and other neglected classes.

Leave it and others in barber shops, waiting rooms, offices, railroad stations, etc.

Make out a list of friends or acquaintances that should read the book; send the book to the first named, ask him to pass it on to the second, and so on.

Suggest to someone the thought of doing "book missionary" work with it and other volumes of the same Series.

Show it to a friend, telling him how good it is, and how inexpensive to circulate.

Call the attention of your local bookseller to it, and urge him to carry a line of the MOODY COLPORTAGE LIBRARY books.

Contents

Introduction

I have been asked by the publishers to write a few lines introducing this book to American Christians. I count it a privilege to be allowed to do so.

The one thing needful for the church of Christ in our day and for every member of it, is to be filled with the spirit of Christ. Christianity is nothing except as it is a ministration of the Spirit. Preaching is nothing except as it is a demonstration of the Spirit. Holiness is nothing except as it is the fruit of the Spirit. These truths are so little taught or emphasized as they should be, and the blessings they speak of are so little experienced, that one gladly welcomes every voice that draws attention to them.

It is known that all do not perfectly agree as to the best answer to the question How to be filled with the Spirit? Some press that aspect of truth which reminds us that the Holy Spirit *has been given* to the church and that He dwells in every believer, a fountain of living water. As there have been fountains clogged by stones and earth, and only needing to be cleared and opened up, so we have only to remove the hindrances, to yield ourselves in perfect surrender to the Spirit in us, and the filling will come. We must not ask God for more of the

Spirit. God asks for more of us that the Spirit may have us wholly.

Others, while admitting fully that the Spirit is in the believer and that He asks for a more entire surrender, yet urge that it is from God directly that the filling of the Spirit must ever still be asked and received. God cannot give His spiritual gifts apart from Himself, once for all. As the divine and everlasting One, He gives unceasingly. The Spirit has not been given as if He had left heaven. He is in God and in the church. It is from God Himself that larger measures of the Spirit must ever be sought and received.

Among those who hold this latter view, there is again somewhat of a diversity in the representation of truth. On the one hand we are reminded that it is *"by faith"* we receive the Holy Spirit, and that faith often has to rest and to act without any conscious experience—has to walk in the dark. Souls that are *fully surrendered* to God are invited to claim the promise and then to go and work in the full assurance that the Spirit is in them and will in His fullness work through them. On the other hand stress is laid on the words *"we receive* the Spirit" by faith. The difference between believing and receiving is pointed out, and we are urged to wait until we receive what we claim, and know that God has anew filled us with His Spirit. "To be filled with the Spirit" is offered us as a definite, conscious experience.

With still other Christians there is to be found what may be regarded as a combination of these different views. They believe that a very definite, conscious filling of the Spirit has been received by some and may be had by all. Though from their own experience they cannot testify of it, they still look for God to do for them above what they have asked or thought. Meantime they know that God's Spirit is in them and seek grace to know Him better and to yield themselves to Him more undividedly. They believe that the Spirit within them is Himself leading them on to the Lord above them, whose it is to fill with the Spirit. They have claimed in faith the fullness; they have placed themselves to be filled; they look to their Lord to fulfill His promise. Whether it comes in one swift moment or more gradually, they know it is theirs.

I have written this with an eye to those who may not entirely agree with the way in which the truth is presented in this little book. I wish to urge all, especially ministers of the gospel, to give it a prayerful reading. I feel confident it will bring them help and blessing. It will deepen the conviction of the great need and absolute duty of being filled with the Spirit. It will point out the hindrances and open up the way. It will stir up faith and hope. And it will, I trust, bring many a one to feel that it is at the footstool of the throne, in the absolute surrender of a new consecration, that the blessing is to be received from God Himself.

And may this book stir up all its readers, not only to seek this blessing for themselves, but to cry earnestly, "praying exceedingly day and night," *"for all saints,"* that God may throughout His whole church give the Holy Spirit in power. It is when the tide comes in that every pool is filled, and all the separate little pools are lost in the great ocean. It is as all believers who know or seek this blessing begin to pray as intensely for each other and all their brethren as for themselves, that the power of the Spirit will be fully known. With the prayer that this Spirit-filled book may be greatly blessed of God, I commend it to the study of His children.

ANDREW MURRAY

London, December 1, 1895

Preface

I have written only for the "babes." The "full grown," the "perfect," who may read will kindly bear this in mind. A wide and more or less intimate acquaintance with the churches of Australasia has shown me the need for a simple, homely talk, such as this little book professes to be. Many, oh, so many of God's dear children are living on the wrong side of Pentecost, living on the same plane as that on which the disciples were living before they "were filled with the Holy Ghost"; and thus by their lives practically making the sad confession, "We did not so much as hear whether the Holy Ghost was given," or "whether there be any Holy Ghost." The object of this little work is to call their attention to their birthright, to the fact that the fullness of the Spirit is the birthright of every believer. God wants us to be living *this* side Pentecost, not the *other* side.

The substance of the following pages has been occasionally delivered as a series of afternoon Bible readings in connection with my mission services. The frequent request that those who heard them might have them in a more permanent form, coupled with the hope that the great blessing that has most graciously been vouchsafed to them when spoken might not be withheld from them when being read, has induced me to commit them to writing.

I gratefully acknowledge help received from many sources, both in preparing the Bible readings and in preparing them for publication; especially do I owe a debt of gratitude to my beloved "fellow worker in Christ Jesus," who has now for many years been "a succorer of many, and of myself also," the Reverend H. B. Macartney, M. A., Incumbent of St. Mary's, Caulfield. He has most kindly revised my manuscript, penned an introduction, and encouraged me to publish.

In "much fear and trembling," because of its inadequateness, but with earnest and unceasing prayer to Him who has been pleased before today to "choose the weak things of the world to confound the things which are mighty"—with the prayer that He would graciously do so again, I send this little messenger forth on its mission, trusting that the reading of it may be as great a blessing to every reader as the writing of it has been to the writer.

Introduction
to First Australian Edition

Christian reader, I pray that before you finish this little book you may become so eager, so intense in your longings after God, that you will not be satisfied until you are really and actually *full* of Him, "filled" with the Holy Ghost.

When the Lord asked Job, "Canst thou lift up thy voice to the clouds, that abundance of waters may cover thee?" (38:34) he would undoubtedly have answered, No. We, on the other hand, with all humility but without the slightest hesitation, can answer, Yes. "Abundance" is the Father's will; abundant are the stores of life in Jesus; "abounding" for ever and ever is the stream of the Spirit's energies.

We have only *to reflect a little* till the truth flashes, and *then* the victory is all but won. We have only to consider *Who* was it that first loved us and called us to be His own children when we were wandering in sin's desert? *Who* was it that first crossed the wild with a cup of living water to slake our dying thirst? *Who* now crosses that desert a second time on our behalf with great camel loads of wine and milk? What did it cost Him to draw that water from salvation's well, or to buy those luxuries for growth and power? What will one healing,

stimulating draught accomplish in us and others? How
will He grieve if we decline to "buy" or hesitate to
"drink"? What, above all, will be the consequences to
His glory?

Oh, let us arise! Let us "shake ourselves from the
dust!" Let us drink abundantly, beloved! There is just
now an unutterable need for "something more." Single
souls are drooping, though divinely planted. Churches
are full of bones, "very many and very dry." The world
is a jungle, a forest ready for the fire. Men, women, and
children form one vast continent of feeling, of ever-
increasing sensibility, with an ever-deepening, an ever-
aching void. Even the teachers of high truth themselves
are not "abundantly satisfied" with the fatness of God's
house; they do not drink deep enough from the "river of
God's pleasures." Yes, there is a thirst not quenched;
and I am persuaded that we can only quench Emmanuel's thirst when *in Him* we quench our own. Then let us
make haste to God; let us hurry to the Stream that is
"full of water." We cannot know what the "Infilling of
the Spirit" means until we are infilled. It is new experience. God is not thereby better seen than before by
nature's eye, but He is better understood, better loved,
better leaned on; that is what He wants, and that is
enough.

Perhaps, dear reader, the pathway between you and
blessing is somewhat hidden, or your eyes are dim, or
your heart is only beating with a faint desire. If so, then
carefully read this little book; read it beside an open
Bible; read it in prayer. It may be, through infinite compassion, that it may prove a key into the "weal thy
place"; it may rend the veil, scatter the darkness, lead
you to joy unspeakable, and—to power!

I have known the author long and love him much. He is thoroughly trained in theology; he is a first rate preacher; his gospel for sinners is as "clear as crystal"; and when you have read a little further, you will say the same of his gospel for saints! He has penetrated far into the "Secret of the Most High" and so can speak from a rich experience of his own, to which, however, he never refers.

I cannot but express the hope that this little treatise on the "Spirit-filled Life" may not only be widely circulated in Australia, but also in England and America. It is fresh, it is homely, it is temperate, it is timely, it is scriptural, it is splendid. It sets forth a promise to be claimed, a gift to be received, a command to be obeyed; and it portrays the sequel—more liberty, more peace, more devotion, more fellowship with the Son of God in His rejection by man, in His fellowship with the Father.

H. B. MACARTNEY, JR.

St. Mary's, Caulfield,
Victoria, July 12, 1894

1

The Starting Point

Reader, are you a B.A.? This little book is only for those who possess that degree from the King's College. If you are not "Born Again," please put it aside, for this is our starting point in considering the fullness of the Spirit as the birthright of every believer. If you have not been born again you have no right by birth to this, the chiefest of New Testament blessings. Your first concern is to become one of the children of God, and then you may inquire as to your inheritance. If you *are* born again, ask that you may read with the anointed eye and with an unprejudiced mind, for the amount of prejudice that exists against this subject is saddening in the extreme.

In nothing that he ever wrote does John Bunyan's masterful genius flash forth more clearly than when, in *The Holy War,* he places that old churl Mr. Prejudice, with sixty deaf men under him, as warder of Eargate. Nothing that even Emmanuel may say can reach Mansoul while Prejudice and his deaf men keep that gate. "There is nothing about this in the Standards of our Church." "I have not met with this truth in my favorite authors." "It is quite new to me, and I never will believe it," etc., etc. These and such like are illustrations one meets with of how well Prejudice keeps his word! In the name of the Lord let us displace him and determine to give what of God's truth may be set forth in the following pages a fair field, no favor being asked for. Deep-rooted prejudice is one of the causes of the appalling spiritual poverty that abounds—yes, appalling when we consider the treasures within our reach.

2

Every Believer's Birthright

On every hand a lack of *something* is being felt and expressed by God's people. Their Christian experience is not what they expected it would be. Instead of expected victory, it is oft-recurring, dreaded defeat; instead of soul satisfaction, it is soul hunger; instead of deep, abiding heart rest, it is disquiet and discontent; instead of advancing, it is losing ground. Is this all Christ meant when He said, "Come unto Me"? Is this life of constant disappointment the normal life of the Bible Christian? To these sad questionings the divine Word answers with an emphatic "No," and the testimony of an ever increasing number of God's children answers "No."

For this widely felt, though sometimes inarticulate demand, the divine supply is the *fullness of the Spirit;* and this fullness is the birthright of *every* believer, his birthright by virtue of his new birth. Sometimes we hear it said that to be filled with the Spirit is the Christian *privilege;* but *birthright* is a stronger word. Reader, it is your birthright to be filled with the Spirit as Peter was filled, as Stephen was filled, as the one hundred and twenty men and women in the upper room were filled (Acts 2:4, 1:14-15), as the men and women in Cornelius's house were filled (Acts 10:44-47). "And ye shall receive the gift of the Holy Ghost, for to you is the promise, and to your children, and to all that are afar off" (Acts 2:38-39).

What have you done with your birthright? Have you claimed it? *Are you living at this moment in the possession and enjoyment of it?* Or are you, Esau-like, "despising your birthright" (Genesis 25:34)? Or, if not despising, are you neglecting it? Esau's eyes were ultimately opened to his folly in parting with his birthright for "one mess of meat," and he then desired to inherit the blessing, seeking it "diligently with tears"; but alas, his awaking came too late (Hebrews 12:16-17).

May every reader of these lines have the desire graciously awakened (if it has not yet been awakened and satisfied) to inherit his birthright blessing while place of repentance is to be found. May the prediction be fulfilled in our glad experience: "The house of Jacob shall *possess their possessions*" (Obadiah 17).

3

A Command to Be Obeyed

But lest some one should think, "It is optional with me whether I claim my birthright or not; no doubt it would be a very fitting thing for some people to be filled with the Spirit, but *I* need not trouble about it"—in case anyone should be tempted to speak and act like this, let us learn that "Be filled with the Spirit" (Ephesians 5:18) is a command to be obeyed, a duty to be done. Many of God's people are acknowledging that they did not know that "Be filled with the Spirit" was a command; *but it is,* and there is no excuse for not knowing.

You will notice that in Ephesians 5:18 there is a double command, a negative, "Be not drunk," and a positive, "Be ye filled." The positive command is as authoritative as the negative and was binding on *just as many* of those Ephesian Christians as was the negative command. Now what was true for those believers there in Ephesus in the long ago is equally true for all believers on God's footstool today.

Is it a sin for a believer today to disobey the command "Be not drunk," and is it then a virtue to disobey the equally authoritative command "Be ye filled"? If it is a sin for a Christian to be drunk, it is just as surely, truly, really, a *sin* not to be filled. We are commanded and expected to live a Spirit-filled life, to be filled, not with wine, the fruit of the vines of earth, but with the new wine of the kingdom, the fruit of the "true Vine."

Reader, if you are asked, Do you obey the command "Be not drunk with wine," what is your answer? If it is "Yes," that is obedience. Now, if you are asked, Do you obey the command "Be filled with the Spirit," what is your answer? If it is "No," that is disobedience; you are guilty of breaking one of God's plainest commandments. You have no more license to break *this* command than you have to break any command in the Decalogue. Before you read further, had you not better confess your sin and tell the Master that you purpose in your heart new obedience?

4

Something Different from the New Birth

This being "filled with the Spirit" is a definite blessing, quite distinct from being "born of the Spirit." Some would object to this and reply that every Christian has the Spirit; quite true, for "if any man have not the Spirit of Christ, he is none of his" (Romans 8:9); and "no man can say Jesus is Lord, but in the Holy Spirit" (1 Corinthians 12:3); but to "have the Spirit" and to be "filled with the Spirit"are two different things. "Egypt always has the Nile," as someone has said, "but Egypt waits every year for its overflow"; having the Nile is one thing, but having the Nile overflowing is quite another. Now it is the Nile's overflow that is Egypt's salvation, and to overflow it must first be filled. So it is the Christian's overflow that is the world's salvation, and in order to have the overflow there must first be the filling.

As far as God is concerned, there is no reason why this filling should not take place at the hour of conversion, of the new birth. See the case of Cornelius and his friends, in Acts 10:44-48. They believed, were saved, "received the Holy Ghost," and were baptized with water the same day. But it were a fatal blunder to assert that *all* men on believing received the Holy Ghost in a similar manner or were thus filled with the Spirit. Most certainly in Bible times it was not so.

THE APOSTLES

In Acts 2:4 we read, "They were all filled with the Holy Spirit," all in the upper room, men and women, including the twelve apostles. Now these men had the Spirit before. When Christ called them to follow Him, when they were converted, they received the Spirit. After His resurrection, but before His ascension, Christ breathed on them and said, "Receive ye the Holy Ghost" (John 20:22), and of course they did "receive" the Spirit then; but it is never said of them that they were "filled with the Holy Spirit" till that morning in the upper room, for the simple reason that it could not be said of them, for "the Spirit was not yet given" (John 7:39). Yet these men were Christians before that morning.

THE SAMARITANS

In Acts 8:5-13 we find that under the preaching of Philip the evangelist there was a work of grace in the city of Samaria, the people believed and were baptized. These people, then, were Christians, but they were not "filled with the Spirit" till Peter and John came down and prayed for them, thus perfecting the work Philip had been doing (Acts 8:15-17).

THE APOSTLE PAUL

Saul was converted when the omnipotent, omnipresent

Christ, standing as Picket-guard for that little church at Damascus, unhorsed him and took him prisoner on the Damascus road. "Lord, what wilt Thou have me to do?" That question sounds like conversion, surely. For three days he lay in darkness in Damascus, a surrendered, believing man, and therefore a Christian man; but it was not till Ananias came to him that he was "filled with the Holy Ghost" (Acts 9:17). And who was this Ananias through whom this man Saul, destined to prove himself the truest, bravest, grandest servant the Lord Jesus ever had—through whom even Saul received the greatest of the New Testament blessings? He was an obscure, obedient believer of whom we know nothing else than that he did this service for Saul. Here is the ministry of the saints. So it may be today, some big Paul may be blessed through the ministry of some little Ananias.

THE EPHESIANS IN ACTS 19:1-6

Here were twelve men who were disciples, they had been believers for some time when Paul found them; in other words, they were saved, they were Christians. But Paul's first question to them was "Have ye received the Holy Ghost since ye believed?" Plainly showing that Paul thought it possible for them to have been believers and yet *not* to have received the Holy Ghost. Indeed, in this case, what Paul deemed a possibility turned out to be a fact; they had *not yet* "received" the Spirit.

Of course, in a *certain* sense, they had the Spirit; it was by the Spirit they had believed, and if they had not the Spirit of Christ, they were none of His; but for all that, they had not yet "received" the Spirit in the Pentecostal sense of the word, in the sense in which Paul meant it. They had not yet come to *their* Pentecost. In the *Revised Version,* Paul's question is rendered, "Did ye receive the Holy Ghost when ye believed?" proving (1) that it is possible to "receive" the Holy Ghost at the moment of believing, and (2) that it is possible to believe without "receiving," as has already been pointed out from the rendering of the Authorized Version. After Paul had instructed them more fully in the word and way of the Lord, we read that "the Holy Ghost came on them." From this we gather that these men of Ephesus obtained a blessing subsequent to their conversion, spoken of here as "receiving" the Holy Ghost, as the Holy Ghost "coming" on them. This is in strict accord with what Paul himself says of this event when writing to the Ephesians in Ephesians 1:13, "After that ye believed, ye were sealed with that Holy Spirit of promise." First, they "believed," and then, some time after "believing," they were "sealed," they "received," they were "filled."

From these four cases—(1) apostles, (2) Samaritans, (3) Saul, (4) Ephesians—we conclude that in New Testament times men actually lived as Christians, were saved, converted men, and yet knew nothing of the "filling" with the Spirit—this knowledge, this blessing coming to them some time after their being born again. Yet this is the very thing some today deny! Whom are we to believe? These objectors or the sacred Record? The divine Word declares it, and there is then no room or need for argument. So we affirm that it is equally possible for believers, for saved, converted men, to live in our own time, as well as in Bible times, without the "fullness"; nay more, it is possible for them to live for years, then die and go home to heaven to be there forever with the Lord, and to have known nothing on earth of what it was to be "filled with the Spirit." But what a loss they have suffered! Eternal, irreparable loss!

So we conclude it is abundantly plain from Scripture that for the regenerate soul there is in Christ another blessing over and above the being born of the Spirit, spoken of as "the fullness of the Spirit." "I am amazed at a man like you going to these conventions," said a man to his minister once. "What new thing can these convention speakers tell you? It is all in the New Testament." "Yes," he replied, "that's the trouble; and we have left these things in the New Testament; whereas we want to get them out of the New Testament and into our hearts and lives."

In Jesus Christ, God's Treasury, our share of Pentecost's blessing has been deposited for each of us by our Father God. Have we claimed and received our share? Not likely, if we are not aware that there *is* such a blessing for us; but once we recognize the fact that it is there, we surely will not rest till we have made it our own. The Scottish bankers have published the fact that they have lying in their vaults a sum of 40,000,000 pounds in unclaimed deposits. Some of those who owned a share of this money may have died in the workhouse; some of them may be living to this moment in direst need, and they might have their money for the claiming; but they do not know that it is theirs. What vast unclaimed deposits are lying in God's Treasury, Christ! Some of His people have died spiritually poor; some are living today in spiritual penury, a hand-to-mouth existence, with such "untrackable riches" lying "at call," on deposit in their name. What have we done with *our* deposit? We are responsible for its use and disuse. Remember the reckoning day is coming (Matthew 25:19).

5

Everybody's Need

Some have the idea that this blessing of the fullness is only for a favored few, for such as have some special work to do for God, but not for ordinary folk "for auld wives and wabsters" in their homespun. Surely this is one of the devil's champion lies! Alas, alas, that it has found such credence! The infilling is what makes this promise true, "He that is feeble among them at that day shall be as David; and the house of David shall be as God" (Zechariah 12:8), so that "one man of you shall chase a thousand" (Joshua 23:10). This means defeat for the devil, so no wonder that he strives to keep us back from the "fullness"!

We are here on earth that through us Christ may be glorified; but there is only one Person that can glorify Christ, and that is the Holy Ghost. "He shall glorify Me" (John 16:14). To the glorifying of Christ as He ought to be and might be glorified the filling with the Spirit is necessary. Mothers in the home, "with thronging duties pressed," need the "fullness" to enable them to glorify Christ as surely as the apostles needed it; the washerwoman needs it as well as the pastor; the trades-man as well as the evangelist. To live the Christ-glorify-

ing life in the station in which God has placed us, we
individually need to be filled with the spirit.

"They were *all* filled" (Acts 2:4), men and women,
the one hundred and twenty in the upper room, the rank
and file as well as the apostles. "Ye shall receive the
gift of the Holy Ghost, for the promise is unto you, and
to your children, and to *all* that are afar off" (Acts 2:38-
39). From Acts 8:17 we gather that *all* the converts in
Samaria, without any favor or distinction "received the
Holy Ghost." From Acts 10:47 we gather that *all* in the
house of Cornelius "received the Holy Ghost" while
Peter was speaking. From Acts 19:6 we gather that "the
Holy Ghost came on" *all* the disciples to whom Paul
was speaking. They *all* received because they *all*
needed. Do not we all need? Why then should we not all
receive? And if we do not receive we will suffer loss,
the church will suffer loss, the world will suffer loss,
and, above and beyond all, Christ will suffer loss.

6

Preventive Against Backsliding

It is most instructive to note how exceedingly anxious the early Christians were that, as soon as a man was converted, he should be "filled with the Holy Ghost." They knew no reason why weary wastes of disappointing years should stretch between Bethel and Peniel, between the cross and Pentecost. They knew it was not God's will that forty years of wilderness wanderings should lie between Egypt and the Promised Land (Deuteronomy 1:2). When Peter and John came to the Samaritans and found that they were really turned to God, their *first* concern was to get them filled with the Holy Ghost (Acts 8:15). When Ananias came to the newly-converted Saul of Tarsus, his first word was, "Jesus . . . hath sent me, that thou mayest . . . be filled with the Holy Ghost" (Acts 9:17). When Paul found certain disciples at Ephesus, his first business with them was to find out if they had "received the Holy Ghost" (Acts 19:2).

These early teachers did not wait for a few months or years till the young converts had become thoroughly disheartened because of the disappointments of the way, thoroughly demoralized by encountering defeats where they had been led to expect that they would come off "more than conquerers"; neither did they wait until the novices had become more established or more fully instructed in the things of God; but straightway, at once, they introduced them to fullness of blessing, taught them the open secret of the overcoming, ever-victorious life, and they did not leave them until the secret was their very own.

Has modern practice been in accord with apostolic practice in this respect? The only possible answer is in the negative. Have we improved then on the apostolic method? Scarcely. But our modern method is very largely responsible for the large percentage of backsliding that one meets within the church today. Many of these backsliders were soundly converted to God, but unfortunately for them, no Peter or John, no Ananias or Paul met them in the beginning of their pilgrimage to compel their attention to the "one thing needful" for the people of the pilgrimage; so they started out but ill provided, and after a longer or shorter time they became thoroughly dispirited; and then asking, "Is this all that is in it?" they threw their profession overboard; and one can scarcely wonder at it.

Prevention is better than cure. Let our young converts be fully instructed and fully equipped with the glorious fullness provided for them by the gracious Father, and we will hear less about backsliding. Do you know why Peter and John, Ananias and Paul spoke of the fullness of the Spirit? Because they possessed and enjoyed the blessing themselves, and they could not but speak of the blessing that had done so much for them.

Do you know why we have not spoken of it to our converts and young Christians? Because we did not know of it ourselves! If we "receive" the Spirit we will "minister" the Spirit; and if we do not "minister," why is it?—but because we have not "received."

7

How Long Between?

It is often asked what time must elapse between the regenerating by the Spirit and the filling with the Spirit. For be it remembered the filling is as real and distinct and definite a blessing as the regenerating. Many people know the moment of their new birth; they were conscious of the change; so also many know when they were "filled with the Holy Ghost"; it was a blessed, bright, conscious experience, and it is as impossible to argue them out of the one experience as out of the other.

On the other hand, some people do not know the time when they were born again; they simply have come to know by many infallible signs that the great change has taken place; so in like manner some do not know when the fullness came to them, but they have been gently awaked to the fact that "Jesus came, He filled my soul"; and such people may be as truly "filled with the Spirit" as those who can tell when and where and how the blessing came to them.

Now as to the period intervening between the two blessings, we know that in the case of the apostles in Acts 2:4, three or three and a half years elapsed between the day when they heard the "Follow Me" and the day when they were "filled"; in the cases of the Samaritans in Acts 8:17 and of the Ephesians in Acts 19:1-7, some weeks; in the case of Saul in Acts 9:17, three days. But as we have already noticed in the case of Cornelius and his household in Acts 10:44, they were regenerated and filled the same day.

From this we gather that, as far as God is concerned, there is no needs-be for any intervening period, but that the believer *may* be "filled" as soon as he is "born again"; the "Life" almost as soon as we get it may blossom into "life abundantly." If we did not "receive the Holy Ghost when" we believed, and if we have not "received" Him since we believed, and are not living now the Spirit-filled life, at whose door then does the blame lie?

8

Other New Testament Names for "Being Filled with the Spirit"

That we may see how full the New Testament is of this blessing, and that we may the better understand what it is and how it is obtained, let us just glance at some other terms used by the Holy Ghost when speaking of it.

"BAPTIZED WITH THE HOLY GHOST"

"Ye shall be baptized with the Holy Ghost not many days hence" (Acts 1:5). See also Acts 11:16, Matthew 3:11, Mark 1:8, Luke 3:16, John 1:33. Now, though "baptized" and "filled" are sometimes convertible terms, it is instructive to note that they are not always so. The promise in Acts 1:5, "Ye shall be baptized," was fulfilled in Acts 2:4, "And they were all filled," where "filled" is used for "baptized." In Acts 4:8 we read, "Peter filled with the Holy Ghost," and in verse 31, "They were all filled with the Holy Ghost," where the word "baptized" could not be used instead of the word "filled."

The difference is this: the "baptism" is received but once; it is, so to speak, the initiatory rite to the life of Pentecostal service, and fullness, and victory. Life begins at the cross, but service begins at Pentecost. If there has been no baptism, there has been no Pentecost; and if no Pentecost, no service worth the name. "Tarry until ye be clothed with power," said the Master (Luke 24:49); "Wait for the promise" (Acts 1:4); "Ye shall be baptized with the Holy Ghost not many days hence" (Acts 1:5); "Ye shall receive power when the Holy Ghost is come upon you" (Acts 1:8). And we see that, in compliance with the commands of their Master, no service of any kind did these men attempt till "the day of Pentecost was fully come" (Acts 2:1).

> Theirs not to make reply!
> Theirs not to reason why!

Their business was simply to *obey*. With the promised "baptism" they entered upon a new phase of life, experience, and service, and this "baptism" need not be repeated; but not so the "filling." Peter was "filled" in Acts 2:4, again in Acts 4:31. The "filling" may be, and ought to be, repeated over and over again; the "baptism" need be but once.

In support of this, note how frequently the word *filled* is used in the Acts and epistles compared with the word *baptized*. The baptism which we are considering here must not be confounded with the baptism in 1 Corinthians 12:13, the "being baptized into one body." Paul is speaking there of every believer having been quickened from the dead by the agency of the Holy Spirit, and thus made a member of Christ's mystical Body. This is a Pauline way of stating the being "born again" of John 3:7. It was to those who already had been "baptized into one body" that Christ gave

the promise "Ye shall be baptized with the Holy
Ghost" (Acts 1:5).

In view then of this word of Christ, "Ye shall be
baptized," and of the word of John the Baptist, recorded in John 1:29-33, "Behold the Lamb of God,
which taketh away the sin of the world . . . the same is
He that baptizeth with the Holy Spirit" (the same
promise is also recorded by Matthew, Mark, and
Luke), it surely cannot be unscriptural for a believer—
painfully conscious that as yet this word has not been
fulfilled in his experience, that for him as yet the day
of Pentecost has not fully come—to pray, "Lord
Jesus, baptize me with the Holy Ghost!" Why should
this be regarded as unscriptural, when in view of the
word, "Be filled with the Spirit," the prayer, "Lord,
fill me with the Spirit," is considered to be in accord
with Scripture? Surely the one prayer in its proper
place is as scriptural as the other! To know Christ as
the Sin-bearer is but *half* salvation; to know Him also
as the great Baptist is *full* salvation. How many there
are who know Christ as their Sin-bearer who have no
experimental acquaintance with Him as the Baptizer
with the Holy Ghost! One cannot think that it would be
grieving to the Holy One that such people should cry
for the promised baptism; but then, when it has been
received, let us bear in mind the difference, already
pointed out, between "baptized" and "filled"; that
now that "the day of Pentecost has fully come," and
that he has been baptized with the Spirit, he must not
continue praying for the baptism, for that cannot be
repeated; whereas he may ask and obtain a fresh filling, a refilling with the Holy Ghost every day of his
life.

"RIVERS OF LIVING WATER"

"He that believeth on Me, as the Scripture hath said, out of his belly shall flow rivers of living water. But this spake He of the Spirit, which they that believed on Him were to receive; for the Spirit was not yet given; because Jesus was not yet glorified" (John 7:38-39). One may ask, What is it to be "filled with the Spirit"? The Teacher Himself makes answer: It is to have "rivers of living water flowing" from one's soul.

See the universality of the promise, "He that believeth on Me"; *no* believer, even the weakest, obscurest, is outside its magnificent sweep, unless by his unbelief he puts himself there. This is not a promise for the spiritual aristocracy of the church, as some, with more heat than sense, maintain. Let us have done with whittling away the vast Godlike promises of the divine Word, till they come within the cramped limits of our poverty-stricken experience, and let us set to work in earnest to bring our experience abreast of God's promises.

This promise is for *you*. Has it then been verified in your life and experience? If not, why not? Is there not a cause? But note more closely its hugeness, its Godlike vastness: "Rivers!" Not a tricklet, or a babbling brook—by its babbling proclaiming its shallowness—or a stream, or a river, but rivers! What divine prodigality! It is the Brisbane, the Clarence, the Hawkesbury, the Murray, the Murrumbidgee, the Tamar, and the Derwent all rolled into one—*Rivers!*

By the widest, wildest stretch of imagination could it be said of you that "rivers of living water" are flowing from you—"flowing," mind you, "flowing"? See the freshness, the freedom, and the spontaneity of the service; no force-pump work about the flowing of the rivers; none of the hard labor of the "soul in prison" (Psalm 142:7). When the "rivers" begin to flow the worker may sell his force-pump; his prayer has been answered, "Bring my soul out of prison."

It is worth noting the gradation in John, chapters 3, 4, and 7. In John 3:7 we have "life" in its beginnings—the new birth. In John 4:14 we have "life abundantly"—"a well of water springing up." The secret of the perennial upspringing is in the word "drink-e-t-h"; "he that drinketh"—not takes a drink, but drinks and drinks and keeps on drinking, is in the habit of drinking—that man never thirsts; for how can a man's soul be dry and thirsty with a well of water in it? Many people are living in the third of John—they have "life," but it is not strong and vigorous; they are suffering from deficient vitality—when Jesus wants them to be in the fourth, enjoying "life abundantly."

The difference between the two experiences is well illustrated in the case of Hagar. In Genesis 21:14 we read that Abraham gave Hagar "a bottle of water" and sent her away. As she wandered in the wilderness "the water was spent in the bottle" (verse 15). But in verse 19 "God opened her eyes, and she saw a well of water." There are "bottle" Christians, and there are "well" Christians. 'Tis a painful experience wandering in the wilderness with an empty bottle and a dying child!

Alas, that there should be so many acquainted with the pain, when all the time God wants us to be independent of any bottle, to be abundantly satisfied with a well of water within us, fed from the hills of God. He wants us to be independent of all but Himself. The "well" is in every Christian, though it is not "springing up" in everyone that has it. The very well, on the side of which Jesus, weary with His long journey from eternity, once sat, has today no thirsty men or women coming to it with their empty pitchers, for the well is dry. How? Why? Because so much rubbish has fallen in that the well is choked. Clear out the well, and the water will spring up again as in Christ's day.

So with many a child of God. The water is within them, the well is there, but it is choked; the water is not springing up, and so they are reduced to dependence on a bottle! Oh, for an anointed eye in our head to see the rubbish, and for grace in our hearts to deal with it, to judge it and to cast it out; and then we would soon have an eye to "see the well of water." May He break every "bottle" and open every eye to see "the well."

Now let us contrast the "well" of the fourth chapter with the "rivers" of the seventh. The "well" is for the supply of all possible *local* needs; but since the Christianity of Jesus is essentially an unselfish thing, He has made ample provision for the supply of *surrounding* needs; "out of him" in whom is the "well"—"out of him" who is abundantly satisfied with Christ—"shall flow rivers of living water," bearing life and satisfaction and gladness into the abounding death and destitution and dreariness that exist on every hand; for "everything shall live whithersoever the river cometh" (Ezekiel 47:9).

Does your church, your neighborhood feel the vivifying, fructifying, refreshing influences of your presence? Most certainly, if John 7:38 is your experience; in other words, if you have been "filled with the Spirit." But remember we must go through the fourth of John to get into the seventh! In John 3 we have the indwelling, in John 4 the infilling, and in John 7 the overflowing.

"THE PROMISE OF THE FATHER"

"Wait for the promise of the Father" (Acts 1:4). See also Luke 24:49; Acts 2:33,39; Galatians 3:14. There are many promises in the divine Word given us by the Father; but there is only one promise spoken of as "the promise," giving it a pre-eminence among all the other "exceeding great and precious promises." What that "promise" was is ascertained by comparing Acts 1:4, "Wait for the promise," with Acts 1:5, "Ye shall be baptized," and Acts 2:4, "They were all filled."

To whom does "the promise" of the Father belong? Surely to all the Father's children without favor or distinction. Since then "the promise is unto you," the question for "you" to settle is, Have you "received" the promise? A promise never made use of is like a check never cashed and is of little use to the one who gets it. Have you cashed the check? If not, why not? The fault is with the child and not with the Father.

"POURING FORTH"

"I will pour forth of My Spirit upon all flesh" (Acts 2:17). See also Isaiah 44:3; Joel 2:28-29; Acts 2:18; 2:33; 10:45. From this expression we may learn still more clearly the copiousness of the blessing.

"THE GIFT"

"And ye shall receive the gift of the Holy Ghost"

(Acts 2:38). See also Acts 8:20; 10:45; 11:17. From his expression may we not learn the freeness of the blessing? In this connection ponder carefully the "how much more" of Luke 11:13.

"Receiving"

"And they received the Holy Ghost" (Acts 8:17). See also, "Ye shall receive power" (Acts 1:8); "have ye received the Holy Ghost since ye believed?" (Acts 19:2); Acts 8:15; John 20:22; Galatians 3:14. Floods of light will be thrown upon the whole subject if we grasp clearly the full force of this expression "receive." "Receiving" is the correlative of "the gift." A gift will not profit one until it is received. It is just here, at the *appropriating*, that we have come short. God has not failed in His "giving," but we have failed in our taking, in "receiving." "Receiving" is a distinct, definite act on our part. Have we "received"? If not, why not? God is "giving."

"Falling"

"For as yet he was fallen upon none of them" (Acts 8:16). See also Acts 10:44, 11:15. From this expression may we not learn the "suddenness" with which the blessing sometimes comes, and comes consciously, too? Compare Acts 2:2, "And suddenly there came from heaven a sound."

"Coming"

"The Holy Ghost came on them" (Acts 19:6). See

also Acts 1:8, John 15:26, John 16:7, 8, 13. From this expression may we not learn the *personality* of the Holy Ghost? "Christ Jesus *came* into the world" and "the Holy Ghost *came* on them" are two parallel expressions. If Christ is here a person, why should the Holy Ghost be a mere influence?

"SEALED"

"Ye were sealed with that Holy Spirit of promise" (Ephesians 1:13). See also 2 Corinthians 1:22. This "sealing" in Ephesians 1:13 is the "receiving" of Acts 19:2, the "coming on them" of Acts 19:6; for here, in this epistle, Paul is evidently referring to the incident related in Acts 19:1-7. In Ephesians 1:13, "In Whom ye also trusted, after that ye heard the word of truth, the gospel of your salvation: in Whom also after that ye believed, ye were sealed with that holy Spirit of promise," we see the successive stages through which the Ephesians passed in their spiritual history. (1) There was a time when they had not heard the gospel; they were living in the darkness of heathenism. (2) Then came the day when they "heard the word." (3) Then they "believed" and were "sealed."

When a Christian is "sealed" by the Holy Ghost, "sealed" as the property of his Master, there will be no need to ask, "Whose Image and superscription is this?" upon the "sealed" one. The King's, of course. Anyone can see the Image. Of what use is a "seal" if it cannot be seen? Is the King's Image visibly, permanently stamped upon us? It is on every Spirit-filled "sealed" believer.

9

How Obtained?

We come now to the practical side of our subject. Surely the unprejudiced reader, if he has not already "received the Holy Ghost," has at least come to the conclusion that there *is* such a blessing mentioned in the New Testament, and lying in God's Treasury, Jesus Christ, for all New Testament believers, and therefore for him—*for me*. Until it dawns on one's consciousness that there *is* such a blessing as "being filled with the Spirit," it is not likely that he will trouble about seeking it, and therefore will never obtain it. In all fairness these terms which we have just been considering—"filled," "baptized," "rivers," etc.—mean *something*. There is *some* blessing represented by the terms, some substance at the back of the shadows. God the Holy Ghost knows what that blessing is. "Have I got *that?*" Is there anything in my life and experience to correspond with *that?* Now comes the question "How am I to get it?" The Bible answer may be summarily comprehended in three words—CLEANSE, CONSECRATE, CLAIM.

10

Wrong Motives

But before proceeding to consider those words, it is absolutely necessary that we be on our guard against desiring this so needful a blessing from wrong motives. We must seek it for one supreme reason—for the glory of God. If self is at the root of our motives at all, God will most surely block our way to fullness of blessing. If we are thinking in our heart of hearts that it would be a good thing for us to get this blessing for our own happiness or satisfaction, or even that we might be more useful, or that in any way we might have the pre-eminence, our eye is not single, our whole body is not full of light (Matthew 6:22).

There is therefore need for the refining fire to go through our heart. God *must* be Alpha and Omega in the matter. "For God's glory, and for God's glory alone" must be our watchword as we proceed with our search after the fullness of the Spirit.

11

Cleansing

As there are conditions requiring to be complied with in order for the obtaining of salvation, before one can be justified, e.g., conviction of sin, repentance, faith; so there are conditions for full salvation, for being "filled with the Holy Ghost." Conviction of our need is one, conviction of the existence of the blessing is another; but these have been already dealt with. "Cleansing" is another: before one can be filled with the Holy Ghost, one's heart must be "cleansed." "Giving them the Holy Ghost, even as He did unto us; and He made no distinction between us and them, *cleansing* their hearts by faith" (Acts 15:8-9). God first cleansed their hearts, and then He gave them the Holy Ghost.

How can we be filled with the Holy Ghost if we are filled with something else? The heart must *first* be emptied and cleansed. The milkman has called on his morning round, and the housewife hears his call. There is a jug standing beside her on the table; it is her own, for she purchased it only last week. She picks it up and looks into it to see if it is clean; she finds it is not. Now she would never think of taking that dirty jug for the milk; but she empties it and rinses and cleanses it, and then, having wiped it dry to her satisfaction, she takes it out for the morning allowance. Indeed, if she brought it out dirty to the milkman, he would positively refuse to put his sweet new milk into it.

So a heart may belong to God, that is, it may be the heart of a Christian man, and yet not a "clean" heart, but until it is cleansed God will refuse to put into it the precious deposit of the "water of life clear as crystal."

A "NEW HEART" NOT NECESSARILY A "CLEAN HEART"

But someone objects, "I thought that when one became a Christian, and was made a partaker of the divine nature, he had a clean heart?" Not necessarily. Many, many a one is born again, is pardoned and justified, and yet has not a "clean heart." "Forgiveness" is one thing, "cleansing" is another, and one may possess the former without possessing the latter. For instance, take the case of David in Psalm 51. He was one of God's people, a restored backslider, when he wrote that psalm. "The Lord also hath put away thy sin" (2 Samuel 12:13), said Nathan to him. But forgiveness, great and sweet as that gift was, was not enough for Israel's now so deeply-taught and penitent King. "Create in me a *clean* heart" (Psalm 51:10), he cries. This is something over and above being "born again," over and above and beyond and deeper even than "forgiveness" (compare Psalm 51:2 and Jeremiah 33:8). See also the New Testament teaching on this point in 1 John 1:7, "The blood of Jesus Christ His Son *cleanseth* us from all sin"; and 1 John 1:9, "He is faithful and just to forgive us our sins, and to *cleanse* us from all unrighteousness." Is the "cleansing" of verse 7 the same as the "cleansing" of verse 9? Most certainly not. The "cleansing" of verse 7 has to do with the *guilt* of sin, with sin after it has been committed; this is the only sense in which the blood of Jesus "cleanses;" it washes white as snow from the guilt and stain of *actual* transgression; that "cleansing" is retrospective. Now, this "cleansing" of verse 7 is the "forgiving" of verse 9; both these words bear on a sinner's justification. But the "cleansing from all unrighteousness" of verse 9 is something different from, something over and above, the "forgiving" of verse 9 or the "cleansing" of verse 7; else, if they mean one and the same thing, would not the author be guilty of tautology? The "cleansing" of verse 9 is prospective and refers to holiness of life, to our being saved from sin, from sinning. And you will notice that it is not the blood of Jesus that does this, but Jesus *Himself* by the exercise of His almighty power.

There is a great deal of confusion on this point in many minds, a confusion fostered, if not begotten, by some of our hymns. Powers are sometimes attributed to the blood of Jesus, to the death of Christ, which belong to Jesus Himself, to the living Christ. We are saved from sin's condemnation by the blood, cleansed from the guilt of all sin, forgiven on the ground of the blood; and in this connection we cannot possibly make too much of the blood, too much of the death of the Son of God—but we are saved from sin's power by Jesus Himself. *"Himself* shall save His people from their sins" (Matthew 1:21). "We shall be saved *by His life"* (Romans 5:10). *"He* is faithful and just to cleanse us from all unrighteousness." The blood "cleanses" in the sense of washing the sin away after it has actually been committed; He "cleanses" in the sense of preventing, restraining from sin. He keeps us back from *sinning*. He "makes us more than conquerors" over sin; and in this so blessed sense "prevention is better than cure."

How often does a mother say to her child when putting on a clean snow-white pinafore in the morning, "Now, my darling, do keep it clean!" "Yes, mother," and she intends to do so; but alas for her intentions! At dinner-time she comes home with her pinafore about as dirty as she can make it. Now, the mother can wash it and make it clean again, as white as ever; but it is weary, wearing work, this everlasting washing. So the Blood of Jesus can cleanse from all sin the garments that are brought to it for cleansing, and what a deal of cleansing it has to do for some of us!

But wouldn't it be just splendid for many a hardworking mother if she could put some power or other into her child—her own self, for instance—by which the child would be kept from making the pinafore dirty at all, so that it would not need washing? Wouldn't this be a vast improvement even on making it clean after it has been made dirty?

This is just what Jesus does. He puts a power within the child that trusts Him—that power is Himself, by which the believer is kept from defiling his garments by any known sin, so that they do not need washing. This is to be "cleansed from all unrighteousness."

But there are whole battalions of God's saved, forgiven, and "cleansed" people ("cleansed" in the sense of verse 7), who are not "cleansed" in this sense ("cleansed" in the sense of verse 9), who are not yet saved from the power of some besetting (that is, upsetting) sin or other.

Have we not known some Christian men who, as has been well said, are like well-supplied cruetstands? Take them which side you like, you will get something either hot or sour, peppery or vinegarish from them! And yet one can scarcely doubt their conversion to God! What are we to say of these cross-grained, or fretful, or worldly-minded, or covetous, or pleasure-loving professors of religion? One would fear to judge some of them and say they were utter strangers to God's regenerating grace; no, but one will say that what they sorely need is the "clean" heart.

WHAT IS A CHRISTIAN HEART?

The question then arises, What is it to have a "clean heart"? What is it to be "cleansed from all unrighteousness"? It is to be "saved from our sins," according to Matthew 1:21. It is to translate 1 John 3:9 into practice, "Whosoever is begotten of God doeth no sin . . . and he cannot sin, because he is begotten of God." It is to have a "conscience void of offense" (Acts 24:16). It is to "know nothing against myself" (1 Corinthians 4:4). It is—in the words of another—to be "saved from *all known, conscious* sin."

But, it is objected, "That is perfection!" (It is amazing how frightened some people are of being perfect! It were well if they were equally afraid of being imperfect; for it is imperfection that grieves God. This dread of perfection has been called by someone "a scarecrow set up by the devil to frighten away God's people from the very finest of the wheat.")

"That is perfection!" Yes and no. It *is* the perfection which is not only allowed but commanded in the Word of God. But it is not *absolute* perfection; it is not sinlessness. Let us look carefully at the expression "From all

known, conscious sin.'' ''From all,'' yes, all, not some
or nearly all, but from ''all known sin''—known, that is,
to us, though not from all known to God; from ''all
known, conscious sin,'' so that one might be able to say,
in the language of the lowliest of the apostles, ''Herein
do I also exercise myself to have a conscience void of
offense toward God and men alway'' (Acts 24:16), and
''I know nothing against myself'' (1 Corinthians 4:4);
or, in the language of the disciple whom Jesus loved,
''We keep His commandments, and do those things that
are pleasing in His sight'' (1 John 3:22).

To have a clean heart, then, is to be saved ''from
our sins,'' saved from sinning, saved by JESUS; note
it well! Not saved by our own efforts, by our watching
and praying, and wrestling and fighting and struggling,
but by Jesus. So it is not a question of what *we* can do,
but of what *He* can do. ''Is anything too hard for the
Lord?'' (Genesis 18:14). Can He not ''guard from
stumbling'' (Jude 24)? Can He not save from sin, from
sinning? Is not this what is meant when it is said, ''He
is able to save to the uttermost'' (Hebrews 7:25)?
''Able to save,'' as Matthew Poole puts it, ''to perfection, to the full, to all ends, from sin, in its guilt, its
stain, its power.''

Yes, He is just as complete, as perfect a Savior from
the *power* of sin as He is from its guilt and stain. He is
equally powerful in each department of His saving work.
But after all is said and done, and one is being saved
from all known, conscious sin, saved from sinning, that
is not to say there is no sin remaining. We are face to
face with the inspired statement ''If we say we have no
sin, we deceive ourselves'' (1 John 1:8). How much sin
may there be in us of which we are entirely unconscious,

but which is naked and open to those "eyes like unto a flame of fire" (Revelation 2:18)!

"I know nothing against myself," cries Paul in 1 Corinthians 4:4, "yet am I not hereby justified; but He that judgeth [examineth] me is the Lord." God may, and does, know much against me when I know nothing against myself; and it is just here that our constant need of the cleansing blood comes in. If the Bible doctrine of the clean heart meant the eradication of sin, a state of sinlessness, that is, absolute perfection, what need would we then have of the cleansing blood at all? Though Jesus Christ may have "cleansed us from all unrighteousness," so that we "have a conscience void of offense," so that we "know nothing against ourselves," yet we need the blood to cleanse from the sins which our eyes fail to detect and of which our conscience takes no cognizance.

It is failure to see this that has led many astray at this point. Having been cleansed and having "no more conscience of sins" (Hebrews 10:2), they imagine they *have* no more sin. How superficial is some people's idea of sin! How little conception have they of the Pauline doctrine of sin! He speaks of sin as "exceeding sinful." How subtle it is! How far-reaching! In their daring ignorance some have actually taken the penknife, like Judah's foolish king, and cut a whole petition out of the prayer which the Lord taught His disciples.

He taught them to pray, "Forgive us our debts as we forgive our debtors"; but these modern lights in their darkness are correcting their Teacher and have cut out that petition and thrown it away. "No need have we to confess our sin, for we have none to confess, and therefore we have no debts to be forgiven." Poor mistaken

people! Never more need of confession and forgiveness
than when they are speaking thus! The holiest of men are
the men who lie the lowest before the Holy One, con-
fessing that which they know only too well (because the
truth is in them) that they "have sin," offering the sacri-
fices with which God is ever well pleased, "a broken
spirit, a broken and a contrite heart" (Psalm 2:17).

The nearer we get to Him "whose head and whose
hair are white as wool, white as snow" (Revelation
1:14), to the Ancient of days "whose garment is white
as snow" (Daniel 7:9), the more conscious are we of
the dullness of our whiteness, of the vast difference
between our whitest and His whiteness; and this consciousness humbles one. "What is it to have sin? What
is sin?" asked a great leader once, and he answered his
own question thus: "It is to come short of the glory of
God; and in this sense we sin every moment of our
lives in thought, word, and deed." Is there a man on
earth who can stand before the infinitely Holy One and
say, "I do not come short of Thy glory"? Should we
speak thus, "we deceive ourselves, and the truth is not
in us."

We may be helped here by observing the difference
between the two New Testament words *blameless* and
faultless. "I pray God your whole spirit and soul and
body be preserved *blameless* [without blame,
unblameworthy], unto the coming of our Lord Jesus
Christ" (1 Thessalonians 5:23). "To present you *faultless* [flawless, blemishless] before the presence of His
glory" (Jude 24).

Now a person or work may be "blameless" and yet
not be "faultless." This is not verbal hair-splitting—by
no means. Suffer a personal illustration. I have lying on

the table beside me a letter which will illustrate the point at issue. I received it when I was away in New Zealand on a mission tour in 1891. It was from my eldest daughter, then a child of five years of age. It reads: "Dear father, I wrote all this myself. I send you a kiss from Elsie." The fact of the matter is, that it is not writing at all, but an attempt at printing in large capitals, and not one of the letters is properly formed; there is not as much as one straight stroke on the page.

Why is it that I prize this letter and keep it laid up among my treasures? Fathers who are as much away from home as I am will understand when I say that it was my child's first attempt at letter-writing. Now, this letter which I prize so dearly is certainly not a "faultless" production; it is as full of faults as it is full of letters, but most assuredly it is "blameless." I did not blame my child for her crooked strokes, and answer with a scold, for I judged her work by its motive. I knew it was the best she could do and that she had put all the love of her little heart into it. She wanted to do something to please me, and she succeeded.

By the grace of the indwelling Christ (for you will perceive that it is His work, "Faithful is He that calleth you, who also will do it," 1 Thessalonians 5:24), this is what our daily life, our daily life-work may be, namely, "blameless"; and He can tell us that it is so, even as I told my child; we may have this testimony, that we are "pleasing God," as Enoch had (Hebrews 11:5).

Oh, the joy! Oh, the inspiration of this God-given testimony! But what a sad mistake for any who may by grace have been made "blameless" to think that they are "faultless," a condition which is to be found only "before the throne." For it is to be noted that the Greek word translated "without blemish," "without fault (*amomos*)" is never used of God's people on earth.

It is used once of the Lamb "without blemish and without spot" (1 Peter 1:19). Elsewhere of the saints:

In Revelation 14:5, "Without fault before the throne of God."

In Jude 24, "Before the presence of His glory without blemish."

In Ephesians 5:27, "That it should be holy and without blemish," when in the sweet by-and-by He will "present the Church to Himself."

In Ephesians 1:4, "Even as He chose us in Him before the foundation of the world, that we should be holy and without blemish before Him in love"; chosen in the past eternity that we should be "holy and without blemish" in the coming eternity, not here, but there; not now, but then; for the word translated "before" is the same Greek word (*katenopion*), translated in Jude 24 "before the presence of."

In Colossians 1:22, "To present you holy and without blemish, and unreprovable before Him." Here he is speaking again of our future standing, for the word translated "before" is the same as in Ephesians 1:4.

"Without blemish" then is sinlessness, having no sin. "And if we say [here on earth] we have no sin [are sinless—blemishless—faultless—flawless], we deceive ourselves [but no one else!], and the truth is not in us" (1 John 1:8). He that has the truth in him knows only too well that he has sin in him, though "cleansed from all sin" by the blood, and though "cleansed from all unrighteousness" by the might of the uttermost Savior. It is most instructive and humbling to notice how the Spirit of truth has placed that

"If we say we have [present tense] no sin, we deceive ourselves," in between His two statements about the "cleansing from all sin" and the "cleansing from all unrighteousness."

But though we will never be able on earth to say with the truth in us that "we have no sin," that we are without blemish, yet the whole Bible teaches us that we may, in this life, be saved "from our sins." (Note the difference between "sin" and "sins.") We may be saved from sinning. "These things write we unto you, that ye sin not" (1 John 2:1): and this is the condition described as "blameless," "unreprovable," "without reproach."

See 1 Corinthians 1:8, 1 Timothy 3:10, Titus 1:6-7, where the Greek word *anegkletos* (unreprovable) is used.

Also 1 Timothy 3:2; 5:7, where the Greek word is *anepileptos* (without reproach).

Also Matthew 12:5, where *anaitios* (guiltless) is used.

Also 2 Peter 3:14, where *amemetos* (blameless) is employed.

Also Luke 1:6, Philippians 2:15; 3:6, 1 Thessalonians 2:10; 3:13, 23, where *amemptos* (without blame) is the word used.

These words describe a state or condition of heart and life which is not only attainable here, but imperative; and the passages we have just been reading prove that it *has* been attained. This is what is meant by a clean heart, to be "blameless," not "faultless."

"I was sitting alone in the twilight,
   With spirit troubled and vexed,
With thoughts that were morbid and gloomy,
   And faith that was sadly perplexed.

"Some homely work I was doing
   For the child of my love and care;
Some stitches half wearily setting
   In the endless need of repair.

"But my thoughts were about the building,
   The work some day to be tried,
And that only the gold and the silver,
   And the precious stones should abide.

"And remembering my own poor efforts,
   The wretched work I had done,
And even when trying most truly,
   The meager success I had won:

"It is nothing but wood, hay and stubble,
   I said; 'it will all be burned;
This useless fruit of the talents
   One day to be returned;

"'And I have *so* longed to serve Him,
   And sometimes I know I have tried;
But I'm sure when He sees such building
   He will never let it abide.'

"Just then as I turned the garment,
   That no rent should be left behind,
Mine eye caught an odd little bungle
   of mending and patchwork combined.

"My heart grew suddenly tender,
   And something blinded mine eyes
With one of those sweet inspirations,
   That sometimes make us so wise.

"Dear child! she wanted to help me,
　I knew 'twas the best she could do;
But oh! what a botch she had made of it,
　The gray mismatching the blue!

"And yet, can you understand it?
　With a tender smile and a tear,
And a half compassionate yearning,
　I feel her grow more dear.

"Then a sweet voice broke the silence,
　And the dear Lord said to me,
'Art thou tenderer for thy little child
　Than I am tender for thee?'

"Then straightway I knew His meaning,
　So full of compassion and love;
And my faith came back to its refuge,
　Like the glad returning dove.

"So, I thought, when the Master Builder
　Comes down this temple to view,
To see what rents must be mended,
　And what must be builded anew;

"Perhaps as He looks o'er the building
　He will bring my work to the light;
And seeing the marring and bungling,
　And how far it is all from right;

"He will feel as I felt for my darling,
　And will say as I said for her,
Dear child! she wanted to help me,
　And love for Me was the spur;

" 'And for the great love that is in it
    The work shall seem perfect as Mine;'
And, because it was willing service,
    Will crown it with plaudit Divine.

"And there, in the deepening twilight,
    I seemed to be clasping a Hand,
And to feel a great love constraining,
    Far stronger than any command.

"Then I knew by the thrill of sweetness,
    'Twas the Hand of the Blessed One
Which should tenderly guide and hold me,
    Till all the labor is done.

"So my thoughts are never more gloomy,
    My faith is no longer dim,
But my heart is strong and restful,
    And mine eyes are unto Him."

A clean heart then does not mean sinlessness, the
eradication of sin, that sin is taken out of us; for though
sin is taken out of the *heart* that is cleansed—for a clean
heart must be clean!—yet "the flesh," the self-life,
remains in the *man,* "latent if not patent," ready to
manifest itself should the counteracting power of the
indwelling Christ the Savior even for a moment be
withdrawn.

This "flesh" is evil (Romans 7:18), and, therefore,
while "the flesh" is in us, "sin" is in us, and hence our
constant need of the cleansing blood. As we trust for
continuous cleansing we get it. "The blood . . . *cleanseth*"—present progressive tense—goes on cleansing,
therefore guilt is never allowed to gather, for as sin

appears the blood cleanses it away and so keeps us clean. Blessed present tense! Thus it is possible for us *always* to walk in the light.

Then as Christ exercises His counteracting power over "the flesh" we are being "cleansed from all unrighteousness," delivered from doing the "not right," and, by continuous trust in our omnipotent Savior, we may know continuous deliverance, continuous victory over sin; we need never know defeat.

A Christian mother had just kissed good-night to her little daughter and was busy in the dining-room arranging the table for dinner, when she heard little feet on the stair. Wondering what was the matter, she slipped into the window recess and hid herself behind the curtains and waited. Presently the little one came into the room and going straight up to some peaches that were on the table, she took one of them away with her! Oh, the agony in that mother heart! She did not speak to her child, but, standing where she was, she spoke to God her Father and asked *Him* so fervently to speak to her child.

God heard that cry, and in a little while the sound of the pattering feet was heard on the stair again. The child came into the room, not knowing her mother was there, and going on tip-toe over to the table she put the peach in the place from which she had taken it. As she turned away with a radiant face, rubbing her hands with delight, her mother heard her say, "Sold again, Satan! Sold again, Satan!"

That's victory! Yes, the cleansing means that and more than that. "We are *more than* conquerors," for when Jesus cleanses the heart, He cleanses the springs of action and being, so that our very desires are purified;

the desire to sin, the "want to," is taken clean away. This is coming off "more than conquerors through Him that loved us" (Romans 8:37). Glory to His name! The man now "wants to" do the will of God. He "likes" what God likes. "I thought you could do what you liked," was the taunt hurled by a young man at a friend of his who enjoyed full salvation on his refusing to go to the theater. "I thought you told me you could do what you liked?" "So I can." "Why, then, won't you come with me as I asked you?" "Because I don't like," was the rejoinder.

The only men on earth who enjoy perfect freedom are the men who have clean hearts, for they not only know that they *ought* to do the will of God, but they *want* to do it, and they *like* to do it, and moreover they have a power that *enables* them to do it. On the other hand, in our jails and hospitals you will find people who thought that they could do as they liked, but they have discovered that they were mistaken.

CLEANSING A CRISIS

But how am I to get this clean heart? Peter answers, "Cleansing their hearts *by faith*" (Acts 15:9). Cleansing is God's work, and the condition on which God will do His work is "faith" on our part. There is only one way of getting anything from God, and that is by faith. One obtained forgiveness and the new birth by faith, and one obtains cleansing of the heart by faith too. You may, you will, get "cleansing" the moment you definitely *trust* Christ for it.

"We aye get what we gang in for" was one of Duncan Mathieson's favorite expressions; and along the line of God's revealed will how true it is! If you will only venture *now* on Christ for "cleansing from all unrighteousness," He will do it for you *now*. "Wilt thou not be made clean? When shall it once be?" (Jeremiah 23:27). Why not *now?* For "cleansing" is a *crisis* and not a *process;* but, as Principal Moule of Cambridge has very tersely put it, "Cleansing is a crisis with a view to a process."

It is just here that multitudes of God's people miss the track. "Sanctification is the *work* of God's free grace." Of course it is; it is a "growth," a gradual process; but "cleansing" is not "sanctification." The latter, in the sense in which it is being used here, is a theological term embracing all the Spirit's work in the believer between the cross and the crown; but "cleansing" is an *act.* While sanctification is a "growth," "cleansing" is one of the conditions of growth, and the very reason why some who hold most tenaciously to the gradual theory of sanctification are "growing in grace" so very slowly is that they have not attended to one of the most essential conditions of growth, namely, this "cleansing."

"But," someone objects, "this is not in the Standards of our church?" That may be; but it is in the Bible. To quote the words of the saintly Dr. Andrew Bonar in another connection, "I believe all that is in our Standards, for I find all that is in our Standards in the Bible; but I believe *more* than is in our Standards, for I find some things in my Bible that are not in the Standards"; for the simple and very obvious reason that you cannot get a quart into a pint measure. While every honest churchman believes that all that is in the Standards of the church to which he belongs is in the Bible, no one in his sane senses believes that *everything* in the Bible is to be found in the Standards. The doctrine of a "clean heart" is one of these things.

In support of the statement that "cleansing" is a crisis, an act, something done in a moment just as conversion is, and not a "process" drawn out indefinitely before one can reach a state of "cleansing," let us ponder well David's prayer in Psalm 51:10, "Create in [margin, for] me a clean heart." Is *creation* an "act" or a "work"? Is it a "crisis" or a "process"? All the Creator had to do was to speak the word, and David's prayer was granted; he then could turn his prayer into thanksgiving; "I thank Thee for having created in me a clean heart"; but he could not thank God for what he had not received. Giving thanks for the clean heart would prove that it was in his possession.

Note also that heart "cleansing" is God's work alone. We are exhorted to "cleanse *ourselves* from all filthiness of the flesh and spirit" (2 Corinthians 7:1), which simply means "separation" from all the palpable, manifest evils Paul had just been enumerating, such as "yoking with unbelievers," "unrighteousness," "darkness," "Belial," "infidel," "idols," "unclean things" (2 Corinthians 6:14-17). In reference to all such things God says, "Cleanse yourselves." The aorist tense is used in the original, denoting a definite, decisive act; "separate from these things at once and be done with them." And where are we to get the enabling power? In effect, God says, "Draw a check on ME; draw on My resources for all you need," for all God's commandings are God's enablings.

But when it comes to be a question of cleansing the "heart," the inner being, the springs of action, that part of the man where the affections and the will are seated, God undertakes that Himself; He says, "Bring that to Me." If this work were left to us it would indeed be a "process" slow and tedious, and progress might be made, as it so often is, alas, backward. But now the question is not what can the believer do by his efforts to overcome indwelling sin, but what can the Almighty God do? It is not a question of our power, but of His.

> " 'Twas most impossible of all,
> That here sin's reign in me should cease;
> Yet shall it be! I know it shall:
> Jesus, look to Thy faithfulness:
> If nothing is too hard for Thee,
> All things are possible to me."

He is able and willing to "cleanse." Are we willing to be cleansed?

Another mistake to be carefully guarded against is this, making "cleansing" to be an *end* instead of a *means* to an end. "Cleansing" is not the blessing that we are seeking; it is only a means. The end is the "filling of the Holy Ghost." "Cleansing" is a negative blessing, the separating from sin; but we can only be satisfied with a positive blessing. When the housewife cleans the house, does she then go out and live in the yard? Not so. She cleans the house that it may be the more fit for her to inhabit. God cleanses, "empties, sweeps, and garnishes" (Matthew 12:44), that He may come in to dwell; and if He, the Holy One, does come in and take up His abode, He will *keep* His dwelling place "clean."

This "cleansing" of which we have been speaking is

one of the steps into the blessed life; but there is not much likelihood of any living the life unless they first take the necessary steps into the life. It is a life of purity, and it is lived, as it is entered upon, by faith in the Son of God; hence the name by which the Spirit-filled life is sometimes called—the life of faith.

12

Consecration: What Is It?

The second step that must needs be taken by those of us who have been living without the fullness before it can be obtained is consecration, a word that is very common and popular; much more common and popular, it is feared, than the thing itself. In order to be filled with the Holy Ghost one must first be "cleansed," and then one must be " consecrated." Consecration follows cleansing, and not *vice versa*. Intelligent apprehension of what consecration is, and of what it involves, is necessary to an intelligent consecration of oneself.

SANCTIFICATION

Consecration is another word for sanctification. Many people have a confused idea as to what sanctification really is. It must be borne in mind that we are not considering the theological term sanctification, but the use of the New Testament word *sanctify, sanctification*. No one would confound "consecration" with "cleansing," and yet many confound "sanctification" with "cleansing."

To "sanctify" is to purify, to cleanse, to make holy, they tell us. But the idea of purification, of cleansing, of

separating from sin is not in the New Testament word
sanctify at all. "The very God of peace *sanctify* you
wholly" (1 Thessalonians 5:23). That does not mean
"purify" you, separate you from sin, as a glance at two
other passages in which the same word occurs will
show. "For their sakes I *sanctify* Myself" (John 17:19).
"*Sanctify* in your hearts Christ as Lord" (1 Peter 3:15,
RV*), where it cannot mean purify, separate from sin.
In these passages its true meaning is very apparent—to
"set apart for a holy use," to "separate to God," to
"consecrate." To "cleanse" is to separate *from* sin, but
to "sanctify" is to separate to God, to set apart for God
that which has already been separated *from* sin. We cannot set apart to a holy use (consecrate) that which is not
cleansed.

Hence we see why it is that "cleansing" must precede
sanctification, or consecration, "that He might sanctify
it, having cleansed it" (Ephesians 5:26, RV). "Sanctification" is not identical with "cleansing," but it is its
complement. "We have been sanctified through the
offering of the body of Jesus Christ once for all"
(Hebrews 10:10). "Wherefore Jesus also, that He might
sanctify the people through His own blood, suffered
without the gate" (Hebrews 13:12). From these passages
we gather that it is by the blood of Jesus we are sanctified, set apart to God. This is another function of the
precious blood in addition to the one we have already
been considering, namely, cleansing from the guilt of
sin.

* *Revised Version.*

SURRENDER

"In conversion," says Dr. Chalmers, "God gives to me, but in consecration I give to God." Everyone knows that conversion should have experimental acquaintance with consecration.

> "In full and glad surrender,
> I give myself to thee."

Consecration, then, involves surrender—total, absolute, unconditional, irreversible. This is Paul's teaching in Romans: "I beseech you therefore, brethren, by the mercies of God, that ye present *your bodies* a living sacrifice, holy, acceptable unto God, which is your reasonable service" (Romans 12:1). These people had already given their souls to God, and now the apostle insists on their giving their "bodies" too. "Yield (RV, present) yourselves unto God as those that are alive from the dead" (Romans 6:13). Life first, then sacrifice. Have we life in Christ? Then it is imperative that we "yield," "present" ourselves unto God. It is not a matter of individual choice or taste or convenience; but everyone that has been quickened from the dead in trespasses and sins is commanded, *yes, commanded,* to "present himself to God." Have *you* obeyed this command? If not, why not? God excuses no one. Had it not better be attended to now? Yes, before you read another line!

It follows as a corollary that if we yield ourselves, we yield everything else to God; nothing is withheld. What loss we suffer because we will hold back some little thing! A little child was one day playing with a very valuable vase, when he put his hand into it and could not withdraw it. His father, too, tried his best to get it out, but all in vain. They were talking of breaking the vase when the father said, "Now, my son, make one more try; open your hand and hold your fingers out straight, as you see me doing, and then pull." To their astonishment the little fellow said, "Oh, no, Pa; I couldn't put out my fingers like that, for if I did, I would drop my penny." He had been holding on to a penny all the time! No wonder he could not withdraw his hand. How many of us are like him! Drop the copper, surrender, let go, and God will give you gold.

Now let us note that the verb translated "yield" (Romans 6:13) and "present" (Romans 12:1) is not in the present tense in the original, as if Paul said "be yielding," "keep presenting," but it is in the aorist tense, the general force of which is a definite act, something done and finished with. So that when the command "Present yourself to God" is complied with as far as one's light goes, the person is entitled to regard the transaction as a completed act and to say, "Yes, I have presented myself to God." Then faith presses on the heels of that statement and says, "God has accepted what I have thus *presented*."

It is absolutely necessary that faith be in lively exercise on this point, for what will be the practical outcome of all my presenting if I do not believe that God takes what I give? "Him that cometh unto Me I will in no wise cast out" is just as appropriate to the saint seeking full salvation as to the sinner seeking pardon. It is failure here, failure to apprehend by faith the fact that God receives what I present, that has blocked progress for so many of God's people who are truly desirous of living consecrated lives. From this it will be seen that consecration is a crisis in the life of the believer, just as cleansing is, and not a process; but it, too, "is a crisis in order to a process."

TRANSFERENCE OF OWNERSHIP

Consecration implies and involves transference of ownership. Many a Christian is living today as if he were his own, but the consecrated heart endorses the statement of the divine Word: "Ye are not your own, for ye are bought with a price: therefore glorify God in your body and in your spirit, which are God's" (1 Corinthians 6:19-20). The consecrated man looks upon himself as the absolute property of the Lord who bought him, and his whole life is lived in the light of this fact.

ENTHRONING CHRIST

Consecration involves the "glorifying" of Christ, the "enthroning" Him, the crowning of Jesus "Lord of all" in our own heart and life. "Crown Him, crown Him, Lord of all"; "and," says Dr. Hudson Taylor, "if you do not crown Him Lord *of all,* you do not crown Him Lord *at all.*" This view of consecration, with its accompanying results, is beautifully illustrated for us in John 7:38-39, "He that believeth on me, as the scripture hath said, out of his belly shall flow rivers of living water. But this spake he of the Spirit, which they that believe on him were to receive: for the Spirit was not yet given; because Jesus was not yet glorified." The flowing forth of the rivers—just the outflow, the overflow of the infilling Spirit—was dependent on Jesus being "glorified." Jesus had not yet reached the throne, and so the Spirit had not yet been given. The reason they had not come to Pentecost was that as yet there was no ascension. Ascension preceded Pentecost. Let us learn it by root of heart, that every Pentecost since the first has, in like manner, been preceded by an ascension.

Do we know Pentecost experimentally for ourselves? If not, the reason is close at hand. Jesus has not been "glorified" by us, not enthroned in *our* hearts. He may be in the heart, He may even be in the throne room, but He has not been placed upon the throne! There has never been a coronation day in our lives, when "in full and glad surrender" we placed the crown on the many-crowned Head, crying, "Crown Him, crown Him, Lord of all!" "And he showed me a river of water of life, bright as crystal, proceeding out of the throne of God and *of the Lamb*" (Revelation 22:1).

When Christ reached the throne at the Father's right hand, from underneath His throne the river began to flow, the Holy Ghost was given, His church received her Pentecost. "Being by the right hand of God exalted . . . he hath poured forth this" (Acts 2:33). So when Christ is "exalted," "enthroned," "glorified" in the believer's heart, from underneath His throne will the rivers begin to flow according to promise; but, no ascension, no Pentecost; and let us remember, as has been already stated, that though life begins at the cross, service does not begin till Pentecost. No Pentecost, no service worthy of the name!

We need not be concerned as to how the rivers are flowing from us, or troubled as to what channels they are flowing in. They flowed from Peter in one way, and from Paul in quite another, and from Barnabas in yet another; there are infinite "diversities" of ways. We need not trouble at all about the rivers and the direction of their flow; our concern is to "glorify Jesus," to see that He is on the throne; and it becomes *His* business then to see that the rivers are flowing; and there is not the slightest danger that the blessed business with which He charges Himself will be neglected!

There are other aspects of consecration in the Divine Word which have not been touched upon, but enough has been said for our purpose to show what it is and what its blessed results will be. Our life and service will be enriched beyond telling by enthroning Christ. This, of course, involves the breaking of all our idols, for He will not share His throne with any. When Mahmoud, the conqueror of India, had taken the city of Gujarat he proceeded, as was his custom, to destroy the idols. There was one, fifteen feet high, which its priests and devotees begged him to spare. He was deaf to their entreaties and seizing a hammer he struck it one blow when, to his amazement, from the shattered image there rained down at his feet a shower of gems, pearls and diamonds— treasure of fabulous value, which had been hidden within it! Had he spared the idol he would have lost all this wealth.

Let us not spare *our* idols. It is to our interest to demolish them. If we shatter them there will rain about our hearts the very treasures of heaven, the gifts and graces of the Holy Spirit; but if we spare our idol we will miss riches unsearchable.

The consecrated life is a Christ-centered life, the only truly-centered life; every other life is eccentric: yet how often do we hear worldly people or worldly-minded Christians (what a contradiction in terms!) criticizing some devoted Spirit-filled man or woman as "so eccen-

tric'' simply because of their loyalty to Christ their
King! When all the while it is the critics that are ''eccentric''—off the true center. Indeed, so eccentric did the
first Spirit-filled band appear that ''others mocking said,
they are filled with new wine''; *so they were* ''full of
new wine,'' the ''new wine'' of the kingdom. And in
God's sight these drunken, eccentric men were the only
truly-centered spiritually-adjusted men in the throng.

13

Claiming

Having considered the two conditions necessary to being filled with the Spirit, namely, the cleansing of the heart and the consecration of the cleansed heart to God, we come now to the very practical question—How is this fullness to be obtained by the cleansed and consecrated believer? Before proceeding to consider the answer, "Claim it," let us notice what the divine Word has to say about (1) prayer and (2) laying on of hands in connection with the obtaining.

PRAYER

"How much more shall your heavenly Father give the Holy Spirit to them that ask Him?" (Luke 11:13.) This promise is given to God's children. It is the dearest wish of the great Father-heart of God that His children should be filled with His Spirit. Who has a fathoming line long enough to sound the depths of that "how much more"? You "ask," Father "gives." What is the next step? Why, of course, you "receive!" Else all Father's "giving" will be of no avail.

"When they had prayed . . . they were all filled with the Holy Ghost" (Acts 4:31).

"Prayed for them, that they might receive the Holy Ghost" (Acts 8:15).

"Tarry" (Luke 24:49). "Wait" (Acts 1:4)—not idling, but praying, pleading the promise, "These all with one accord continued steadfastly in prayer" (Acts 1:14).

"They were all with one accord in one place, and suddenly" the answer came (Acts 2:1)! So in obtaining the blessing of the Fullness, prayer has its place.

LAYING ON OF HANDS

"Then laid they their hands on them and they (the Samaritan converts) received the Holy Ghost" (Acts 8:17).

"Then when they had fasted and prayed, and laid their hands on them, they sent them away" (Acts 13:3). Barnabas and Saul were men who were already full of the Holy Ghost, but by the laying on of hands (it is probable that hands had been laid on these men before this) they received a fresh anointing of the Holy Ghost, a fresh equipment for special service, and thus they were set apart for the work to which the Holy Ghost was calling them.

"And when Paul had laid his hands upon them [the men of Ephesus], the Holy Ghost came on them" (Acts 19:6).

"They laid their hands on them [the deacons]" (Acts 6:6).

"Neglect not the gift that is in thee, which was given thee by prophecy, with the laying on of the hands of the presbytery" (1 Timothy 4:14).

"Stir up the gift of God, which is in thee through the

laying on of my hands'' (2 Timothy 1:6). It is quite evident that laying on of hands was no meaningless ceremony in the primitive church. Is there any reason why it should ever be an empty, barren form in our own day?

We come now to examine the answer given to the question—How is the fullness of the Spirit to be obtained?—namely, ''Claim it.'' It must be borne clearly in mind that we are dealing now with a cleansed and consecrated soul. If you are not ''cleansed,'' attend first to the cleansing. If you are not consecrated, attend at once to the consecrating, and then (but not till then) will you be able to profit by what will be said about the claiming of the blessing.

Do we appreciate the immense difference between ''claiming'' and ''asking''? I ''claim'' that which is mine own; I ''ask'' for a favor. For instance, if a man has a credit balance of $250 in his current banking account and draws a check for $50, he does not require to go to the manager and ''ask'' for $50; he presents his check and ''claims'' it, for it is his own. But supposing that same man is in need of an advance of $500; he goes into the manager's room, and ''asks'' for the favor of a loan. No ''claiming'' now!

So it is often with the Christian and his God. When God gives him a definite promise for some definite blessing, it is the Christian's privilege to ''claim,'' to ''receive'' by faith the thing promised. If God tells him a certain blessing is his by virtue of his sonship, it is his to ''claim,'' to ''receive'' what through grace has been made his own. There is no ''asking'' needed here, that is, ''asking'' in the sense of saying—''Lord, *if* it be Thine holy will, give me this.'' Where is the room for an ''if''? Has not God told him it *is* His will?—has He not promised it?—has He not given it to him? Why, then, should he mock his Lord by saying, "If it be Thy will"?

But supposing, on the other hand, that that man wants something which God has not expressly promised to give, something in reference to which He has *not* revealed His will; all the Christian can do in this case is to "ask"; he cannot "claim"; and God *may* give him what he asks, or He may see that it will be for the best to refuse His child's request. A Christian may want $250 and may "ask" his Father to send it to him, and God may give or withhold. But if a Christian man wants to be filled with the Holy Ghost, he need be in no doubt as to the issue here, he may "claim" the fullness, for has not God promised it? Is not this blessing his very own? His birthright by virtue of his new birth? Let us learn then clearly to distinguish between "claiming" as an act of faith based on an express promise in the Word, and "asking" as a request in prayer.

That the fullness of the Holy Ghost is one of the blessings which it is our privilege to "claim," to "receive" by a simple act of faith, is abundantly clear from the Book of God. "Christ hath redeemed us from the curse of the law, being made a curse for us; for it is written, Cursed is every one that hangeth on a tree: that the blessing of Abraham might come on the Gentiles through Jesus Christ; that we might receive the promise of the spirit *through faith*" (Galatians 3:13-14).

The double purpose of Christ's redeeming work, of His being made a curse for us, is here plainly stated. He was "cursed" that we might be blessed with a double blessing—(1) with "the blessing of Abraham," that is, righteousness, justification; and (2) with "the promise of the Spirit." How many of God's children forget the second blessing!—they think that if they are saved from wrath and justified, that that is all!—but that is only half salvation; full salvation consists in receiving the promise of the Spirit in *addition* to being justified. Have *we* overlooked this fact? Have we been stopping short at half salvation?

Those who are not living the "Spirit-filled life" are making void to a most alarming extent, as far as they are concerned, the work Christ accomplished on the tree. Christ died that we might be made the righteousness of God *and* that we might be filled with God. As God holds the sinner guilty who neglects so great salvation and rejects the offered righteousness, so He holds the justified believer guilty who neglects the second blessing which Christ purchased with His Blood, namely, the offered "promise of the Spirit."

But note well how Paul tells us this latter blessing is to be made ours; it becomes ours *"by faith."* No one doubts how we receive the blessing of Abraham (righteousness, justification); all are agreed that it is "by faith." "Being justified by faith" (Romans 5:1). But how blind we are to see, how slow to take it in, in spite of the plain declarations of Scripture, that "the promise of the Spirit" is in like manner received "by faith"! The Holy Ghost is the "gift" of the Father and of the Son (Luke 11:13). This "gift" is received "by faith." There is the whole matter in a nutshell. Of all the sublime things in God's sublime Book there is surely not a sublimer than this, that a cleansed and consecrated believer may by simple faith *here* and *now* claim and receive the fullness of the Spirit—the greatest gift that even the exalted Christ has in His power to bestow upon His people.

"Be filled with the Spirit," saith the Holy Ghost. Note that the command is in the passive voice, "Be filled," that is, "Let yourself be filled." The fullness is pressing in upon you, only let it in! Receive it, and it is yours! *Have you got it?* If not , deal with the Lord about it at once, somewhat after this manner, "Lord Jesus, Thou dost command me to be filled with the Spirit. I take Thy command and make it my prayer, 'Lord, fill me with Thy Spirit.' Thou hast told me that 'all things whatsoever ye pray and ask for, believe that ye have received them, and ye shall have them' (Mark 10:24). It is Thy desire to fill me; it is my desire to be filled. I have made, 'Lord, fill me,' the prayer of my heart. I claim the fullness. I believe for it. I receive it now by faith. I *have* received it. I have it. It is mine, Lord. I thank Thee for filling me, even me, with Thine Holy Spirit." And the blessed business is done!

It is yours to believe, to receive. It is *His* to fill. Go on your way now, reckoning that you are filled, and God will make the reckoning good. It is *yours* to *keep believing*. It is God's to *keep you filled*. Stagger not at the promise of God through unbelief, but be made strong in faith, giving glory to God. Some object to this quick, almost instantaneous, and easy way of receiving this greatest of the New Testament blessings. But every objection urged against receiving the fullness of the Spirit in this way applies with equal if not greater force to a sinner receiving the pardon of his sins when he comes to God at the first. It is always in grace that God deals with the sinner and justifies him the instant he believes in Jesus. It is always in grace that God deals with the justified one and fills him with the Holy Ghost the moment he receives the fullness by faith. Eternal life

is the gift of God, and all the sinner has to do is to take
it.

The Holy Ghost is a gift, and all God's child has to do
is to take it. But some will still object and say that it is
necessary to spend some time "waiting" on God for the
fullness before we can get it. A night of prayer, or a half
night at least, a more or less protracted season must thus
be spent before we can hope to receive the blessing we
desire. Of course not one word can be uttered against
spending seasons of prayer by day or by night in waiting
upon God. We have the example of the Man of Prayer
Himself before us in this. But this much must be said,
that many a one has spent whole days and nights and
weeks in earnest crying to God for the infilling of the
Holy Ghost, and all in vain.

All in vain? Why? How? *Because of unbelief.* If you
want to fill a corked bottle with water and take it to a
running tap, but neglect to remove the cork, how long
will you have to wait holding it under the tap before it is
filled? Remove the cork, and the bottle is running over
in a few seconds! Many a one has cried and waited and
waited and cried for the fullness of the Spirit, but the
stopper of unbelief has been in their empty hearts, and
so no wonder that they did not get what they wanted! Of
what avail will all God's "giving" be if a man does not
"receive"? God cannot *give* and *receive* too!

But someone may still object, and, in proof of his
contention that we must "wait" for the filling of the
Holy Ghost, point to the case of the disciples, who continued in prayer for ten days, waiting for the promise of
the Father. Quite true that they "waited"; but it must be
remembered that that prayer meeting was ante-pentecos-
tal; *we* live in post-pentecostal days; *they* were waiting

for the Spirit to come from heaven. "The Spirit was not yet given." We have not so to wait. He *has* come, He *has* been given, and all we have to do is to receive Him.

We have read of Christ's coming into the world and of His leaving it. We have read of the Spirit's descent, but we do *not* read of *His* ascension. A Christian man came to me once and said—expecting a word of encouragement and approval—"I have been seeking that blessing for over thirty years." "Brother, it's nearly time you got it then!" was the swift rejoinder. For all these years during which the man was crying, "Give, give, give!" God was saying, "Take, take, take! Receive, receive! for I *do* give!"

If I heard my little girl of three years old crying piteously for a piece of bread, knowing that she must be very hungry and having the bread by me, would I tell her to cry on for another hour and that then I might attend to her wants? "How much more," oh, *"How much more* will your heavenly Father give the Holy Spirit to them that ask Him?" But what if, in spite of her crying and of my offering, she would not take the bread I offered but still went on with her crying, "Father, oh, father, do give me a piece of bread. I am so hungry!" You silly child! Oh, how many silly children has the Father in His family, crying year in and year out, "Give, give!" and Father all the while yearning over them and saying, "Take, take, My child!" Let some of us give over crying and set to work "receiving." Take and thank! Receive and thank! "That we might receive the promise of the Spirit *through faith.*"

14

How Does It Come?

How does the filling of the Spirit come? "Does it come once for all, or is it *always* coming, as it were?" was a question addressed to me once by a young candidate for the baptism of the Holy Ghost. There are many asking the same question. We have considered how the fullness is obtained, but now we proceed to consider, How does the fullness come?

In speaking of the blessing of being filled with the Spirit, the New Testament writers use three tenses in the Greek—the aorist, the imperfect, and the present. Each of these tenses has a different shade of meaning. The inspiring Spirit has employed these different tenses for a purpose, and it will be to our profit to try and get at that purpose, to note the differences, and to learn His meaning.

(1) The aorist tense—a tense to which the English language is a stranger—denotes generally "a sudden, definite act of the past," "something done and finished with"—"They were filled"—as in Acts 2:4.
(2) The imperfect tense, denoting, as in English, just what its name implies—"They were being filled" (literally)—as in Acts 13:52.

(3) The present tense, also denoting, as in English, just
what its name implies—"Full," the normal condition—as in Acts 11:24.

The following are the passages in the Acts in which
the various tenses are found:

(1) *Aorist:*

Acts 2:2, "It filled all the house."

Acts 2:4, "They were all filled."

Acts 4:8, "Peter filled with the Holy Ghost." Peter
was already "filled" (Acts 2:4).

Acts 4:31, "And they were all filled with the Holy
Ghost." Peter was again amongst them. Peter received
an "aorist" filling in Acts 2:4, 4:8, and 4:31. So that an
"aorist" filling may be repeated and repeated again and
yet again. On two occasions—4:8 and 4:31—there was
special need, and to meet this special need Peter
received a fresh and special and definite "filling" of the
Holy Ghost. From this we learn that to equip us for
every new important or difficult service to which we
may be called, the Lord Jesus is prepared to grant us a
fresh infilling, a "refilling" of the Holy Ghost; and that
these "refillings" may be, and ought to be, repeated just
as often as the need arises. We see it reported twice in
one chapter that Peter was "refilled." It will be noted
that for the reasons already mentioned, the expression "a
fresh infilling of the Holy Ghost," or "refilling," is
used instead of "received a fresh baptism of the Holy
Ghost."

Acts 9:17 (Saul), "And be filled with the Holy
Ghost." Saul was not to begin his life work until "baptized"—"filled with the Holy Ghost." He must receive
the very same blessing and equipment as the other apos-

tles received at Pentecost. This was Saul's Pentecost, and for him, as for others, service began at Pentecost.

Acts 13:9, "Paul filled with the Holy Ghost." The man who was filled in chapter nine of Acts is "filled" anew in this passage, the "aorist" blessing is repeated, fitting him for the special work on hand, namely, administering that scathing rebuke to Elymas the sorcerer. In all these passages the blessing is spoken of as a crisis, not as a process.

(2) *Imperfect:*

Acts 13:52, "And the disciples [literal] *were being filled* with joy and with the Holy Ghost." This is the only passage in the Acts where the imperfect tense is used. It is not the aorist "were filled," but the imperfect "were being filled," implying the inflow, not only to make up for, but to sustain, the outflow. The same idea of the "imperfect" is seen in Ephesians 5:18, "Be filled with the Spirit," where Principal Moule points out that the Greek verb rendered "be filled" may with equal correctness be rendered "Be ye *filling* with the Holy Ghost." The preceptive verb "is in the Present or continuing tense; it enjoins a course, a habit," so that in this sense "the fullness" is *always* coming, it is spoken of as a process, not as a crisis.

(3) *Present:*

Acts 6:3, "Look ye out therefore, brethren, from among you seven men of good report, full of the Spirit and of wisdom, whom we may appoint over this business," men whose normal condition was "full" of the Holy Ghost. It is well worth noticing the business for which these "deacons" were wanted; they were to look after temporal affairs, to feed a few decent old Greek widows; and yet even for this business the men must be"full of the Holy Ghost"! None other need apply. How far has the church of today strayed from apostolic practice! When an election of office bearers is taking place nowadays, of men, say, to manage the temporal affairs of Christ's church, who ever thinks of looking out for "men full of the Holy Ghost"? Many a man is elected to office in the church of the living God who "has not the Spirit of Christ" at all—who is therefore not a child of God, much less "full of the Holy Ghost." "He is a man of social position, a man of means; if he is not full of the Holy Ghost, he is at least full of this world's goods, and you know he will be a pillar in our church." Yes, as someone has well remarked, he will be a *cater*-pillar!

The church of the New Testament does not need pillars of that kind. The church of Jesus Christ and His apostles does not require to be propped up by children of the devil. What right have we to ask an "alien," a man who is "without Christ," "having no hope and without God in the world," to assist in managing and controlling the Father's house? Such was not apostolic practice. "Be ye not unequally yoked together with unbelievers" (2 Corinthins 6:14). What an amount of unequal yoking there is in many of our churches, although the church's Lord expressly forbids it! "Thou shalt not plough with an ox and an ass together" (Deuteronomy 22:10). Who is responsible for this unequal yoking? Is it not the church members that elect these men and put them into office in the church of God? Church members, beware! Next time offices are to be filled in your church, whether they have to do with the temporal affairs or with the spiritual, remember apostolic advice, "Look ye out from among you men full of the Spirit." When we get back in this matter to apostolic practice, we may hope to get back apostolic blessing, but not till then.

Acts 6:5, "Stephen, a man full of faith and of the Holy Spirit." In those brave days of old it was a case of demand and supply. Wanted—seven men full of the Holy Ghost; and immediately they were forthcoming! Is the trouble nowadays in the demand or in the supply? In both. The demand for Spirit-filled men is very slack; but even if the demand revived tomorrow, how lamentably few in our churches could be found bearing the trade mark as "up to sample"! Still there are not wanting signs of revival in both demand and supply. Let us remember that Stephen's companions were men full of the Holy Ghost, although Stephen is the only one of whom it is expressly stated. He was the most remarkable man of the seven, a man in whom the graces of the Spirit shone with conspicuous brightness. So mighty was his faith that special mention must needs be made of it. It is not sufficient to describe him as a man full of the Holy Ghost, but it must be stated that he was "a man full of faith *and* of the Holy Ghost." Faith was his outstanding grace.

Acts 7:55, "He being full of the Holy Ghost." This was Stephen's normal condition right up to the very end of his life; it was true of him when we get our first glimpse of him, true also as he passes within the vail into the unspeakable glory.

Acts 11:24, Barnabas "was a good man and full of the Holy Ghost." A good man indeed, and so full of the Spirit of God that there was no room for self; for we read that he came into the midst of a great revival, in the bringing about of which he had no hand, and instead of being filled with envy at the divinely-chosen instru-

ments, instead of picking holes in the work and depreci-
ating the whole movement, he was filled with gladness;
we read that he "was glad" (11:23). It goes without saying that *that* man was "full of the Holy Ghost." How
many there are nowadays who are not like Barnabas.
Having now considered the passages in which the various tenses are used, we are able to answer the question—How does the blessing come? Does it come once
for all, or is it always coming? There are sudden definite
"fillings," repeated with more or less frequency; times
when the believer is conscious of being "filled," when
he can say, "I was filled."

Between this experience—"filled" (which is an
"aorist" blessing)—and that which should be the normal
experience of every Christian, namely, "full" (which is
a "present" blessing), it is evident that there is a great
gap; but God has graciously bridged the gap for us; the
connecting link between the "aorist" *were filled,* and
the "present" *full,* is the "imperfect" *"were being
filled,"* so that the blessing is always coming. Does it
come once for all? A thousand times no!—if by that is
meant that we are reservoirs into which the fullness is
poured, so that once we are filled, we are independent of
fresh supplies from the Lord Jesus. That surely were a
curse instead of a blessing! What reservoir is there that
does not need replenishing? Some Christians say that at
times after some piece of service has been finished, they
feel as if they were empty, as if their souls had been
quite drained, and now they are dry and thirsty. It need
not be so. It is not so with the Spirit-filled worker whose
faith is in lively exercise, for he is "being filled" all the
time.

In driving between Melbourne and my home I often

stop at a wayside trough to give the horse a drink. I notice that the trough is quite full of water and that there is a box in one end of it. As the horse drinks the water is lowering, and presently I hear a sound as of a running tap. Yes, the sound is coming from the box. That box is covering a piece of mechanism that needs explaining. Within it there is a tap connected by pipes with the Yan Yean Reservoir up in the Plenty Ranges. Attached by a lever to the tap is a metal ball, which rests on the surface of the water. As the horse drinks, the water on which the ball is floating is lowered, and thus the ball is lowered; the lowering of the ball opens the tap and the Yan Yean begins to pour in; so that, although the water is being withdrawn by the thirsty animal, a fresh supply is being poured in, the trough is "being filled," so that it is always "full."

Thus may it be with the soul of the believer. No matter what the outflow into the surrounding emptiness may be, or the withdrawals by thirsty, needy souls, there is the continual inflow, so that there may be the constant "fullness." Indeed the outflow depends directly on the inflow; one can only give as he gets. It is ours to see to the connection between us and the infinite Reservoir away up among the hills of God being kept open, to see that the tap is kept in proper working order by faith and prayer and meditation, and then, one might almost say automatically, the heart will be kept full, "filled with all the fullness of God," no matter what the spiritual drain upon us may be; for now it is not a question of our capacity to contain, but a question of God's infinite supply for all our needs. This too is the explanation of the "overflow," the flowing "rivers" of John 7:38. It is the overflow, and only the overflow, that blesses. There is not a drop for thirsty souls till someone overflows. It is the overflow in the Sabbath school class, and in the pulpit, and, for that matter, in every other sphere of Christian service, that brings blessing; and this overflow is in direct proportion to the inflow. "Rivers" cannot flow out unless "rivers" first flow in.

An ordinary service pipe in our domestic water supply may serve to illustrate some of the points we have been considering. We take a bucket to the tap for water, and lo, there is none. Something is wrong. Either the authorities have cut off our supply because of some infraction of the law on our part, or there is an obstruction in our service pipe, or the pressure is insufficient to give us even a drop, or the supply is so deficient that it has been shut off for a time from us that it may be sent in another direction. Sometimes, alas, the "flowing" of the "living waters" from the soul of the believer ceases; but the ordinary round of duty, either in the district visiting, or in the Sabbath school class, or in the pulpit has not ceased; a ceaseless stream of *talk* may still be flowing on, but there is no "living water" in it all. Why?

It is not that the pressure aback of us, the pressure in the infinite Reservoir away up among the hills of God, is insufficient, or that the supply is deficient, unable to meet our needs because it is supplying needy ones elsewhere. God's water supply never breaks down as we often find our city supply failing. If the "flowing" has ceased, it is from one of two reasons: either God has, in mercy and in judgment, cut off the supply, or there is an obstruction in us, and *sin* is at the bottom of both reasons. "Search me, O God . . . and see if there be any way of wickedness in me" (Psalm 139:23-24). "Confession, cleansing" is the divinely-appointed method for putting right what has gone wrong.

Sometimes on going to the tap we find that there is water but such a miserable dribble, either from insufficient pressure or some partial obstruction in the pipe, or perhaps it is because we have not opened the tap fully. What a wretched parody of the flowing "rivers" of John 7:38 are the life and service of many of the Christians of today! Some of the "living water" is doubtless coming from them, but it is only percolating through, dribbling, trickling out of them. Why?

Certainly not, as has been already remarked, from insufficient pressure; the fault, the failure is not on God's side, but there is some local obstruction—amounting in many a case to almost entire obstruction—some little idol or other in our heart, if not a "sin," yet certainly a "weight" (Hebrews 12), and this hinders the outflow. Confession and cleansing are still God's remedy. Or the hindrance may be our unbelief, "limiting the Holy One of Israel"; opening the tap but a little instead of opening it full; expecting little when we were divinely authorized to expect much; refusing to obey the command "Open thy mouth wide, and I will fill it" (Psalm 81:10). "Rivers" cannot flow through a heart full of unbelief.

Sometimes, again, on going to the tap we get a little water and a great deal of air. What a noise! Now air is a very good thing in its own place, but that is not in a water pipe; that is meant to convey water and nothing else, and for the water pipe to do its work, it is necessary that it be emptied and cleansed of everything else, even of air. Scripture hath said that some things "puff up," and there is a good deal of "puff" in some hearts through which the living water is supposed to be flowing. God be merciful unto us! Such hearts, like our water pipe, need emptying and cleansing.

Yet once more, on going to the tap, we find a splendid supply; the pipe is clean, the pressure is good. Now before we open the tap the pipe is full of water; when the tap is opened and the bucket filling, the pipe is still full, for although the water is pouring out at the tap, it is pouring in at the reservoir, so that the pipe is *kept* full, even though the tap is open and the water streaming from it. When the tap is shut, you cannot say any more about the pipe now than that it is still full of water.

Even so may it be with the believer who is spiritually adjusted. When resting at his Master's feet he is full; when actively engaged in service he is still full; his normal condition is "full of the Holy Ghost," because he has learnt how to obey the command "Be ye filling with the Spirit."

15

Its Effects

Among the effects and benefits which in this life accompany and flow from being filled with the Holy Ghost may be mentioned the following:

COURAGE

"Oh, I could not do so and so—I have not the courage," is a reply frequently made by Christian people when asked to undertake some piece of service or other for the Master. The first point to be settled is, "Is that the Master's will for me?" If so, lack of courage is a confession to the lack of the "fullness of the Holy Ghost." The Spirit-filled man knows the fear of God and knows no other fear.

Acts 2:14, "Peter, standing up with the eleven, lifted up his voice and spake forth." No fear of servant maids now! But *can* this be the man who quailed before the look of the waiting-maid who charged him with being "with the Nazarene"? Can this be the man that "began to curse and to swear, I know not this man of whom ye speak"? The very same, and yet not the same; for the baptism of the Holy Ghost has changed Peter the craven-hearted into Peter the lion-hearted, so that he can stand

before that surging multitude, their hands dyed crimson
in his Master's blood, and without a tremor charge home
upon them the awful crime "Him ye did crucify and
slay."

Acts 4:13: "They beheld the boldness of Peter and
John."

Acts 4:31: "They spake the word of God with
boldness."

Acts 5:20: "Go ye and stand and speak in the temple." Taken out of prison and ordered to go and do
again the very thing for which they had been impris-
oned! But they were Spirit-filled men, and so we read in
the next verse, "They entered into the temple."

Acts 5:29: "We must obey God rather than men."

Acts 5:40-42: "Beaten . . . departed rejoicing . . .
ceased not to teach."

Acts 21:13: "I am ready not to be bound only, but
also to die at Jerusalem, for the name of the Lord
Jesus." Courage-filled because Spirit-filled!

THE FRUIT OF THE SPIRIT

The fruit of the Spirit will be manifest in the life: love,
joy, peace, etc. (Galatians 5:22-23). How can one's life
be filled with the fruit of the Spirit unless one's heart is
first filled with the Spirit Himself? In the primitive
church the men and women were filled with the Holy
Ghost; that was the rule; now, alas! it has come to be the
exception—and as a consequence we see how their lives
were enriched by the fruit of the Spirit.

Love: Acts 4:32, "Were of one heart and soul . . . had
all things common." This may be poor political economy, but it is good spiritual economy, a simple Bible

illustration of the Bible precept "Lay up for yourselves treasure in heaven" (Matthew 6:20). If brotherly love were abroad today, how soon the present distress would disappear! As the best available commentary on this heavenly word *love,* study on your knees the whole of 1 Corinthians 13.

Joy: Acts 2:46, "They did take their food with gladness and singleness of heart, praising God." Every meal was a sacrament. The same cause would produce the same result today.

Acts 5:41: "Rejoicing that they were counted worthy to suffer dishonor for the Name," when some of us would have been bemoaning ourselves and complaining of the hardness of our lot!

Acts 13:50-52: "Stirred up a persecution . . . and the disciples were [being] filled with joy."

Acts 16:25: "Paul and Silas were praying and singing hymns unto God." The heavier the tribulation the more their joy seemed to "overflow" (2 Corinthians 7:4), and of course the heavier the tribulation the more joy they needed to sustain them. "For the joy of the Lord is your strength" (Nehemiah 8:10).

Peace: Acts 6:15, "Saw his [Stephen's] face as it had been the face of an angel."

Acts 7:59-60: "They stoned Stephen, calling upon the Lord, and saying, Lord Jesus, receive my Spirit, and he kneeled down, and fell asleep."

2 Corinthians 4:8-9: "Troubled on every side, yet not distressed; perplexed, but not in despair; persecuted, but not forsaken; cast down, but not destroyed."

Thus we might go through the heavenly list—longsuffering, gentleness, goodness, faith, meekness, temperance—and see how richly in Bible times the fruit flourished in the lives of those who were Spirit-filled. Before passing on let us notice where it is that joy grows. It grows between love and peace. It is, as someone has well called it, a sheltered fruit. If love withers, joy is exposed on that side, and it too will fade. If peace is interfered with, even though love is vigorous, joy is exposed on that side now, and it will fade away and die. The only way to preserve joy in vigorous growth is to see that its sheltering fruits, love and peace, are kept free from blight, and vigorous too.

In his letter to the Ephesian church, to whom he addressed the command "Be filled with the Spirit," Paul points out very clearly in chapters five and six what the results of the fullness will be.

(1) A singing heart (5:19). This is what would bring us and our lives up to concert pitch. We would no more go "flat." This would drive away the leaden dullness.

(2) A thankful heart (5:20). Such a heart would not be finding fault with Christ's government; will "find none occasion of stumbling in" Jesus (Matthew 11:6); will not be offended at Him, no matter how He may test and try it. "Blessed is he" that has such a heart in his bosom!

(3) A submissive heart (5:21), "in lowliness of mind each counting other better than himself" (Philippians 2:3). " The thing [once] impossible shall be."

(4) Spirit-filled wives will be in subjection to their own husbands (5:22).

(5) Spirit-filled husbands will love their wives as Christ loved the church (5:25).

(6) Spirit-filled children will obey their parents (Ephesians 6:1).

(7) Spirit-filled fathers will not provoke their children to wrath (6:4).

(8) Spirit-filled servants [bond-slaves] will be obedient to their masters (6:5).

(9) Spirit-filled masters will treat their servants as they [the masters] would wish to be treated by *their* Master (6:9).

Would not results (8) and (9) be the best possible solution of the constantly recurring labor and capital difficulty and render a labor war impossible, because unnecessary?

(10) Spirit-filled men will be strong in the Lord, spiritual giants, not sickly, hunchbacked dwarfs (6:10).

(11) Spirit-filled men will be warriors, clad in the whole armor of God; if not Spirit-filled they could not carry it (6:11).

(12) Spirit-filled soldiers will not be warring against flesh and blood; internal foes having all been subdued, the civil war has ceased; their enemies are now external, and they are free to concentrate all their attention and God-inspired energies on them. Their enemies are (1) in the world—principalities and world-rulers and (2) in the heavenlies—powers and spiritual hosts of wickedness (6:12).

(13) Spirit-filled men will be praying always in the Spirit (6:18). In order to do this vigilance is necessary "watching thereunto."

Such are some of the results, on the positive side, of being filled with the Spirit. The effects on the negative side are manifest in Galatians 5:16-17, "Walk in [by] the Spirit, and *ye shall not fulfill the lust of the flesh.* For the flesh lusteth against the Spirit, and the Spirit against the flesh; for these are contrary the one to the other: that ye [walking by the Spirit] may not do the things that ye would'' (if ye were walking by the flesh). (See Galatians 5:19-21.)

Another effect of a Spirit-baptized church would be that the *masses would be reached*. See how the early church—which was a Spirit-baptized church and persistently kept that truth in the foreground—reached the masses, and with what blessed results! They were not amused or entertained, but they were converted, saved, turned to the Lord.

"There were added unto them in that day about *three thousand* souls," Acts 2:41.

"The number of the men came to be about *five thousand,*" Acts 4:4.

"Added to the Lord *multitudes* both of men and women. . ." Acts 5:14.

"The number of the disciples *multiplied* in Jerusalem exceedingly, and a *great company* of the priests were obedient to the faith," Acts 6:7.

"The *multitudes* [in Samaria] gave heed with one accord unto the things that were spoken," Acts 8:6.

"And *all* that dwelt at Lydda and in Sharon saw him, and they turned to the Lord," Acts 9:35.

"It became known throughout all Joppa; and many believed on the Lord," Acts 9:42.

"While Peter yet spake these words, the Holy Ghost fell on *all* them which heard the word," Acts 10:44.

"And the hand of the Lord was with them: and a *great number* that believed, turned unto the Lord," Acts 11:21.

"And the next Sabbath almost the *whole city* was gathered together to hear the word of God," Acts 13:44.

"And so spake that a *great multitude* both of Jews and of Greeks believed. . ." Acts 14:1.

"And when they had preached the gospel to that city, and had made *many* disciples. . ." Acts 14:21.

"The churches . . . *increased* in number daily," Acts 16:5.

"These that have turned *the world* upside down are come hither also," Acts 17:6.

"Crispus . . . believed . . . and *many* of the Corinthians hearing believed," Acts 18:8.

"So *mightily* grew the word of the Lord and prevailed," Acts 19:18-20.

We often hear of discussions on the "lapsed masses." "Why have the masses of the people lapsed from the churches?" Perhaps the more correct way of putting it would be, Why have the churches lapsed from the masses? The answer is not far to seek—because they have lost the driving power which alone could keep them abreast of the masses, even the baptism of the Holy Ghost. The conditions were just as unfavorable in the first century as in the nineteenth, and yet we read, "So mightily grew the word of the Lord and prevailed." It is positively painful to see the substitutes that are being tried today for the power of the Holy Ghost. Miserable substitutes are they all. One church is trying this plan, another that, and not one of them has found a new plan that is a permanent success. They are floundering, and some of them are foundering, and no wonder. It will be no loss to the kingdom of God if churches which ignore the Holy Ghost should founder.

Let us get back to Pentecostal methods. The trouble is that the churches have lost their way to that "upper room." Let a church only find her way back there and obtain her Pentecost; let pulpit and pew be baptized with the Holy Ghost *and with fire,* and the people will come running in to see the burning. That church will not need to cater for amusements as a bait to catch the masses, but the people will come crowding into her pews, climbing into them as Zacchaeus climbed into the branches of that sycamore tree when he wanted to see the Lord; for the people still want "to see Jesus," and they have heard that He is "to pass that way." We cannot improve on Pentecost's methods for reaching the masses.

PERSECUTION

Yet another effect of the fullness of the Spirit must be mentioned, namely, persecution.

"Others *mocking* said, They are filled with new wine," Acts 2:13.

"They laid hands on them and put them in ward," Acts 4:3.

" Let us threaten them," Acts 4:17.

"They laid hands on the apostles and put them in public ward," Acts 5:18.

"And were minded to slay them. . ." Acts 5:33.

"They beat them and charged them not to speak," Acts 5:40.

"And seized him and brought him into the council," Acts 6:12.

"And they stoned Stephen," Acts 7:59.

"And there arose on that day a great persecution," Acts 8:1.

"Haling men and women committed them to prison. . ." Acts 8:3.

"Saul, yet breathing threatening and slaughter against the disciples of the Lord. . ." Acts 9:1.

"Took counsel together to kill him. . ." Acts 9:23.

"They went about to kill him," Acts 9:29.

"Killed James the brother of John with the sword. . ." Acts 12:2.

"He put him [Peter] in prison," Acts 12:4.

"Stirred up a persecution against Paul and Barnabas. . ." Acts 13:50.

"Made them evil affected against the brethren. . ." Acts 14:2.

"To treat them shamefully and to stone them. . ." Acts 14:5.

"They stoned Paul," Acts 14:19.

"Commanded to beat them [Paul and Silas] with rods. . ." Acts 16:22.

"Cast them into prison . . . and made their feet fast in the stocks. . ." Acts 16:23-24.

"Set the city on an uproar. . ." Acts 17:5.

"Stirring up and troubling the multitudes. . ." Acts 17:13.

"Opposed themselves and blasphemed. . ." Acts 18:6.

"Rose up against Paul, and brought him before the judgment seat. . ." Acts 18:12.

"Speaking evil of the way. . ." Acts 19:9.

"Filled with wrath. . ." Acts 19:28.

"No small stir concerning the way. . ." Acts 19:23.

"A plot was laid against him by the Jews," Acts 20:3.

"So shall the Jews at Jerusalem bind the man that owneth this girdle, and shall deliver him into the hands of the Gentiles," Acts 21:11.

"And laid hands on him. . ." (Paul was never free after this) Acts 21:27.

"As they were seeking to kill him. . ." Acts 21:31.

"Beating Paul . . . bound with two chains . . . into the castle. . ." Acts 21:32-34.

"It is not fit that he should live," Acts 22:22.

"Bound themselves under a curse, saying that they would neither eat nor drink till they had killed Paul. . ." Acts 23:12.

"They delivered Paul . . . to a centurion," Acts 27:1.

"From henceforth let no man trouble me: for I bear branded on my body the marks of Jesus," Galatians 6:17.

All this makes lively reading in this peaceful, easy-going day of ours; and yet the world has not changed in its attitude or feeling towards God and the things of God. But a most palpable change has taken place some-where. The change, alas, is in us, in the people of God; a change that is not for the better. We have lost that which brought these men into direct collision with the world and with its ways, even the fullness of the Spirit. Only let a man in our day seek and obtain the blessing that made these men mighty for God, and he will soon find that the world has not changed and that the "Phari-sees" have not changed either; the fullness of the Holy Ghost makes a man the uncompromising friend of God, and that certainly involves the enmity of the world. "Therefore the world hateth you" (John 15:19).

It behooves those who are seeking the "fullness of the Spirit" to remember these facts and to count the cost, for the persecution may come from the most unlikely, unlooked-for quarters. To be forewarned is to be fore-armed. "In the world ye have tribulation: but be of good cheer; I have overcome the world" (John 16:33).

16

May One Know that He Is Filled?

The question is often asked—How am I to know when I am filled with the Holy Ghost?

The Testimony of the Written Word

"All things whatsoever ye pray and ask for, *believe that ye received* them, and ye shall have them" (Mark 11:24). From this you know that if you have, up to your light, fulfilled the conditions necessary to the filling of the Holy Ghost, on praying and asking for the fullness, it is your privilege to believe that you have received that you have asked for; nay, it is your bounden duty, in compliance with Christ's express command, to so believe. If God gives, and you really receive, you may then give thanks, and that proves that you possess, for you cannot truly give thanks for what you do not possess! It will be noted that this answer is precisely similar to the answer that would be given to the question—How am I to know that I am saved? By simple faith on the testimony of the Word. As multitudes have accepted salvation without any emotion, without any feeling whatever, so many a one has accepted by faith the "fullness of the Holy Ghost," without any wave of emotion or feeling bearing witness to the fact of the filling. But this is not to say that there is never any feeling, that the emotions are never stirred; not so, for the feelings will come in due course, in God's own time.

THE WITNESS OF THE SPIRIT

Again, one may know that the fullness has come by the witness of the infilling Spirit. Just as in multitudes of cases the blessed Spirit bears witness with the blood when it is applied at the moment of conversion, so many a one knows in his inner consciousness the moment when the fullness of the Spirit was bestowed; they felt the incoming and can date their baptism, as others have felt the regenerating change and can date their conversion.

It should also be repeated here, that as many are ignorant of the date of their conversion, though well assured of the fact, so many may be ignorant of the date of their baptism with the Holy Ghost, though well assured that they have entered on the blessed life. If we are assured of the fact that we have received the fullness of the Spirit, we need not worry as to dates.

THE SIGNS FOLLOWING

Yet again, one may know whether the fullness has come to his heart and life by the signs following, by what "The Men" of the North of Scotland would call "the marks." Christ's words used in another connection may surely be applied in this, "By their fruits ye shall know them" (Matthew 7:20). "The fruit of the Spirit is love, joy, peace, longsuffering, gentleness, goodness, faith, meekness, temperance'' (Galatians 5:22-23). The fullness of the fruit will surely be found where the fullness of the Spirit is. Quantity and quality will both be there. As this has already been touched upon when considering the effects of the blessing, no more need be added here. But this, however, must be clearly borne in mind, that, while the fullness of the Spirit is a *gift*, the fruit of the Spirit is a *growth*. Fruit grows, and the fruit *will* grow, if only we see to it that the conditions are present which are favorable to growth. That man does not manifest much wisdom who expects full growth without attending to the conditions of growth.

17

May One Say that
He Is Filled?

The question has been raised—Is it right for one to *say* that he is "filled with the Holy Ghost"? May this not savor of egotism? John said of Jesus—"Behold the Lamb of God, who taketh away the sin of the world . . . the same is He that baptizeth with the Holy Spirit" (John 1:29, 33). Christ's twofold office here is to "take away sin," and "to baptize with the Holy Spirit." Each one who knows Christ as the "Sin-bearer" should have an experimental acquaintance with Him as the "Baptizer" too. Indeed, this alone is *full salvation*. To have sin taken away is but half salvation; to be "baptized with the Holy Spirit" as well is to possess full salvation.

Now, if Christ has taken away a man's sin, may that man not know it? Certainly. And if he knows it, may he not bear witness to the fact? Nay, does Christ not expect him to confess?—to tell what great things the Lord hath done for him? No right thinking person would regard it as wrong for a saved man to confess his Savior or would regard his confession as egotism. By parity of reasoning, if Christ has baptized a pardoned man with the Holy Ghost, may that man not know it? Surely! And if he knows it, may he not bear witness to the fact? May he not tell what still greater things the Lord hath done for

him? Would this be wrong? Must *this* necessarily be
egotism? At the same time, while it is perfectly scriptural for a Spirit-filled man to testify, for Christ's glory,
as to the infilling of the Holy Spirit when questioned
upon it—for we must be careful not to libel the grace of
God that is in us and not to grieve the Holy Spirit by
ignoring Him or His work within us—one cannot be too
careful lest he be found casting his "pearls before the
swine" (Matthew 7:6), and as a rule it will be better in
this matter to let the life speak rather than the tongue.
Indeed it will not often be necessary for the Spirit-filled
man to be questioned on the subject at all; his speech
will betray him, his manner of life, his fruitful service.

18

May One Lose the Blessing?

The question trembles from many a lip—If I get the blessing, may I lose it? Most certainly. But, glory be to God! He has made ample provision for failure. There is no reason why we *should* fail; God has made ample provision *against* failure; we must not expect to fail; *but* in case we do fail, provision has been made. The most prolific cause of loss is disobedience—disobedience either to one of God's written commands or to the inward promptings of His Holy Spirit. "The Holy Ghost whom God hath given to them that obey Him" (Acts 5:32).

This all-glorious gift is not only obtained but retained in connection with obedience. It is absolutely necessary to maintain the attitude of complete self-surrender, for the slightest act of disobedience—that is, the asserting of our own will in opposition to His will—may cost us the loss of the blessing, such as neglecting to speak to a man about the great salvation, or refusing to give a tract to someone when we knew God wanted us to do so. We must learn to be obedient to the promptings of the Spirit. "Mine eyes are ever toward the Lord" (Psalm 25:15) must be our constant attitude.

If we possess the blessing and desire to retain it, there is another matter of the last importance that must be attended to, namely, letting "the Word of Christ dwell in you richly in all wisdom" (Colossians 3:16). The Spirit-filled man will be a Word-filled man. A neglected Bible is responsible for much of the lost blessing from which many of God's children are suffering today. If we would retain the blessing in its fullness and freshness, we must feed *daily* and feed *much* upon Christ as He is revealed to us in the Holy Scriptures. It is the function of the indwelling Spirit to take of the things of Christ and to show them unto us (John 16:14). He does not speak from Himself or of Himself but of Jesus; and so He will be continually drawing us to the Word, that He may have the opportunity of drawing our attention to fresh beauties in Immanuel.

There is much so-called reading of the Bible that is not "searching the Scriptures" (John 5:39), not "delighting in the law of the Lord," not "meditating in it day and night" (Psalm 1:2), not "letting the Word of Christ *dwell in you richly.*" You cannot live a Spirit-filled life and be content with a shallow, meager acquaintance with the divine Word. The Spirit-filled man gives God's Book its own proud place, the premier place, in all his reading. It is instructive to compare the effects of being filled with the Spirit and of being filled with the Word. "Be filled with the Spirit; speaking *one to another in psalms and hymns and spiritual songs, singing and making melody with your heart to the Lord*" (Ephesians 5:18). "Let the word of Christ dwell in you richly in all wisdom; teaching and admonishing *one another with psalms and hymns and spiritual songs, singing with grace in your hearts unto God*" (Colossians 3:16).

Have we then, unhappily, through disobedience or

neglect, lost the blessing which once we possessed? Is there one saying, "Oh, that I were as in the months of old!"? (Job 29:2). It may be "all joy" with you again, for if you have lost the blessing, just go back and search for it, and you will find it where you lost it! Just there and nowhere else. Have you found the spot where your obedience failed? Yield and obey just there, pick up your obedience where you dropped it, and there you may obtain the blessing again as you obtained it at the first; but *just there and nowhere else.*

An illustration of this is found in 2 Kings 6. The divinity students of those days were going down to build a new Divinity Hall on the banks of the Jordan, and they asked Elisha, the man of God, to go with them. The story tells us that as one of the students "was felling a beam, the axe-head fell into the water; and he cried and said, Alas, my master, for it was borrowed. And the man of God said, Where fell it? And he shewed him the place. And he cut down a stick, and cast it in thither; and the iron did swim. And he said, Take it up to thee. So he put out his hand and took it," and having re-fixed the axe-head on the handle, he went on again with his felling (6:5-7). Where was it that the student got his lost axe-head? Where he lost it, in the very spot where it fell into the Jordan's waters—it was just *there* that he found it. So if you lose the blessing, the only spot on earth where you need look for it, if you wish to take it up to thee again, is *the very spot where you lost it*. Let us all learn by root of heart what the student did *not* do. After the axe-head flew from the handle, he did not continue at work chopping with an axe-handle. No; but as soon as he lost his axe-head, he *stopped till he got it on again*.

Oh, that many a Christian worker would read, mark,

learn, and inwardly digest! Then some Sabbaths there might be many a pulpit without a preacher, and many a Sabbath school class without a teacher, and many a sphere of Christian labor without its worker. Why? Where are they? Away looking for their axe-heads? Away to the banks of that river of disobedience in whose sluggish waters they lost them! Alas, that there should be so many today with an axe handle, trying in this way to fell beams for the house of our God, working with the blessing lost! Hard labor this, and very little to show for it—except earnestness! "And isn't it a fine thing to be in earnest?" Yes, but it is a finer to have a little of that uncommon thing—homely common sense—at the back of the earnestness, and the man who is hewing with an axe-handle doesn't impress one as being overburdened that way!

If we have enjoyed and have lost the fullness of the Spirit, let us confess, betake us to the open fountain and obey, and He will put away our sin: and then let us start afresh, let us come to Him again for the fullness as at the first, and we will find that "He abideth faithful: for He cannot deny Himself" (2 Timothy 2:13). For the sake of the sacred Heart, for His Name's glory, for the sake of souls, and for our own sake, we must not, we will not, try to live and labor without being

"Filled with the Spirit."

Moody Press, a ministry of the Moody Bible Institute, is designed for education, evangelization, and edification. If we may assist you in knowing more about Christ and the Christian life, please write us without obligation: Moody Press, c/o MLM, Chicago, Illinois 60610.